from THE ATTIC
lost photos

Marjorie J. Levine

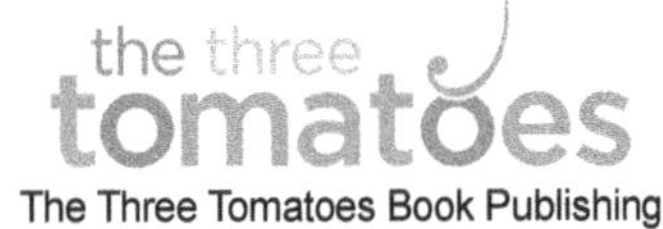

The Three Tomatoes Book Publishing

Published February 2022

ISBN: 979-8-9856298-1-1
Library of Congress Control Number: 2022902043

For information address:
The Three Tomatoes Book Publishing
6 Soundview Rd.
Glen Cove, NY 11542

Cover Photo: Frederick Piccarello
Author's Photo: Frederick Piccarello
Interior photos courtesy of Marjorie J. Levine
Cover and interior design: Susan Herbst

for Alan Berliner who inspired me to find
creative ways to preserve personal old photos
and
for the Bumph

DIRTY LAUNDRY

These opening pictures are of my parents and their friends.
They were taken over eighty years ago during a road trip.
I am gobsmacked at how they were inspired to create for photos
bold layers of humor around discovered remains and
I am amused at how they continued a naked theme
in several snapshots as the years passed.

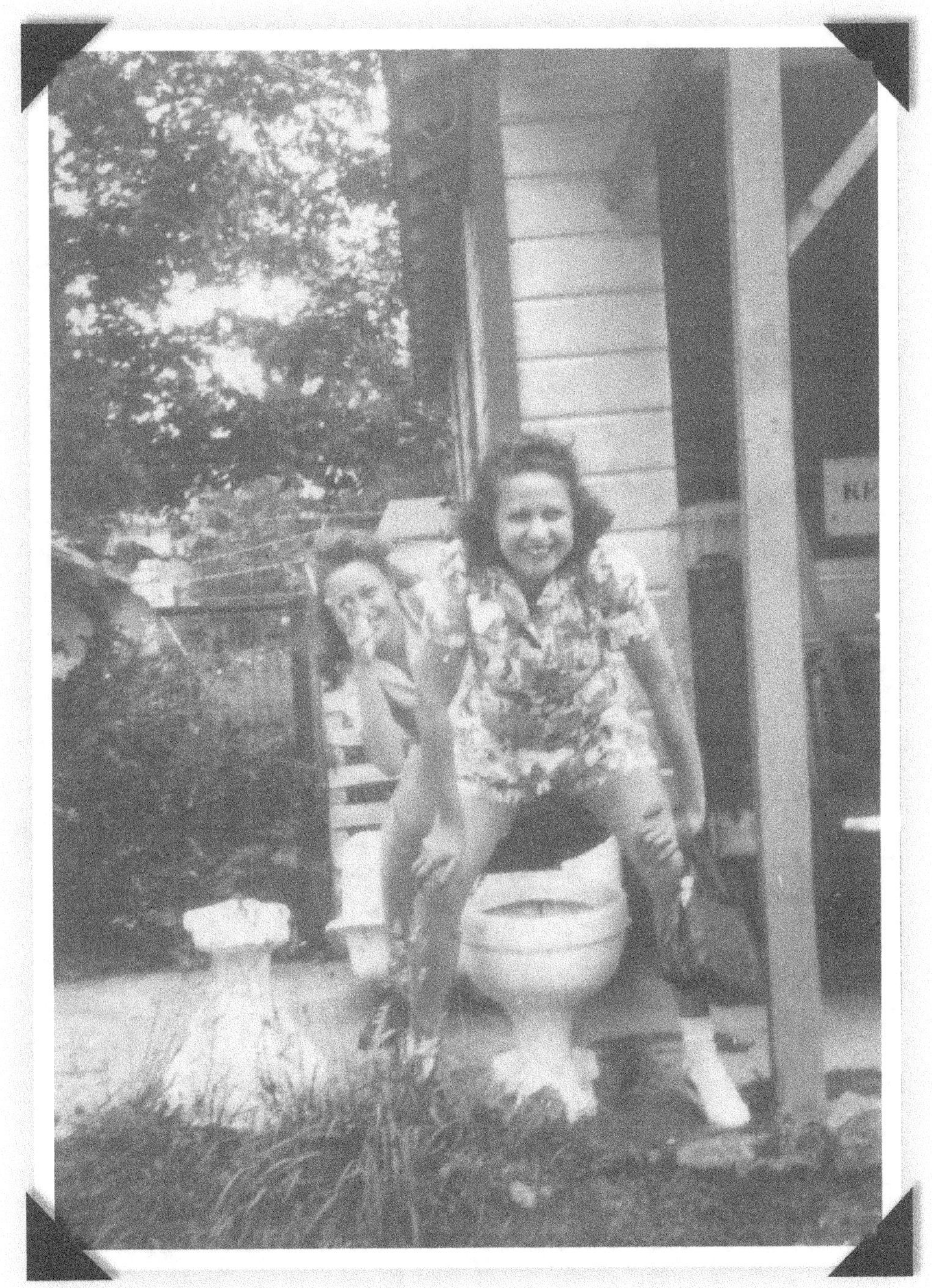

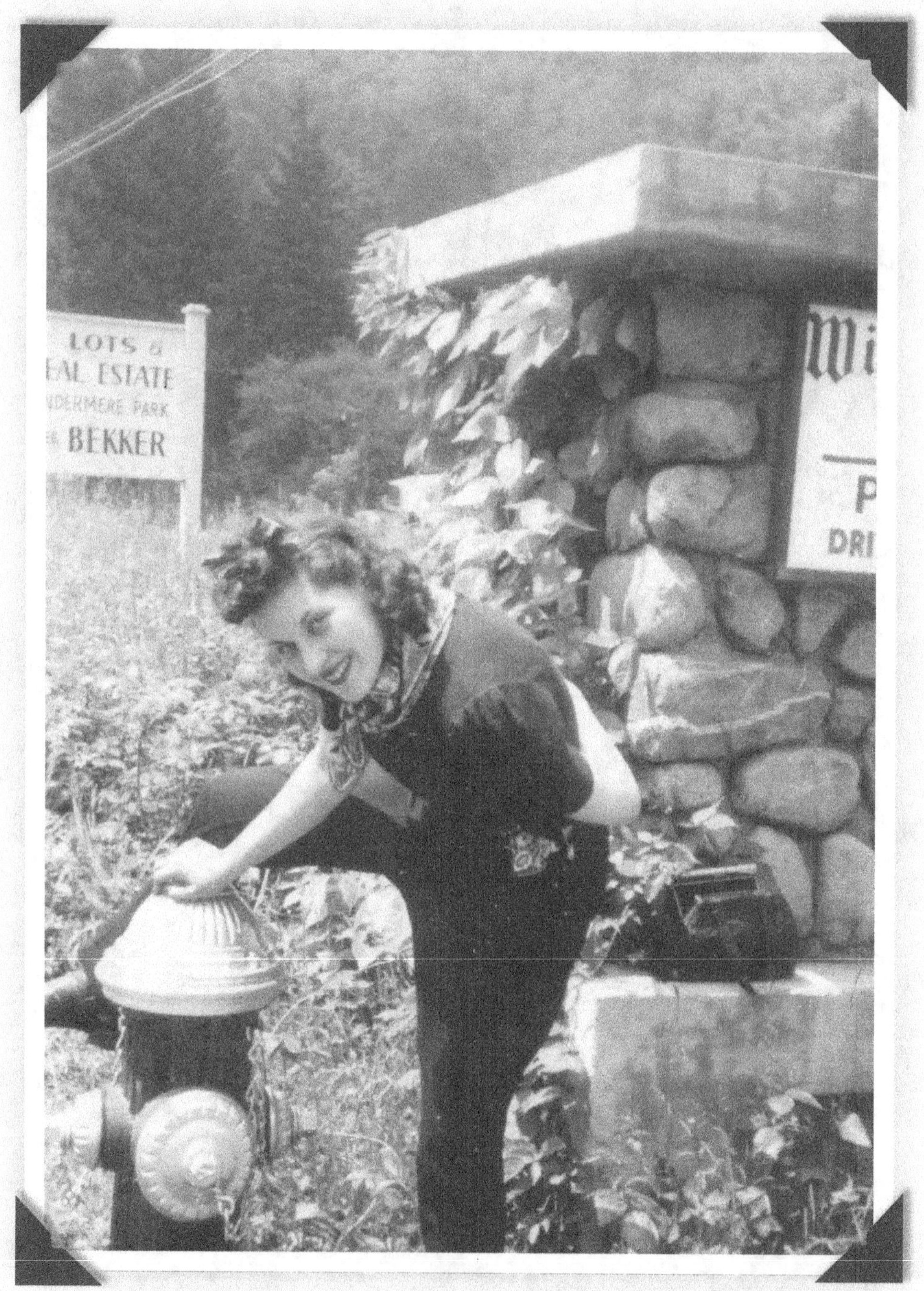
LOTS &
EAL ESTATE
NDERMERE PARK
BEKKER
Wi
P
DRI

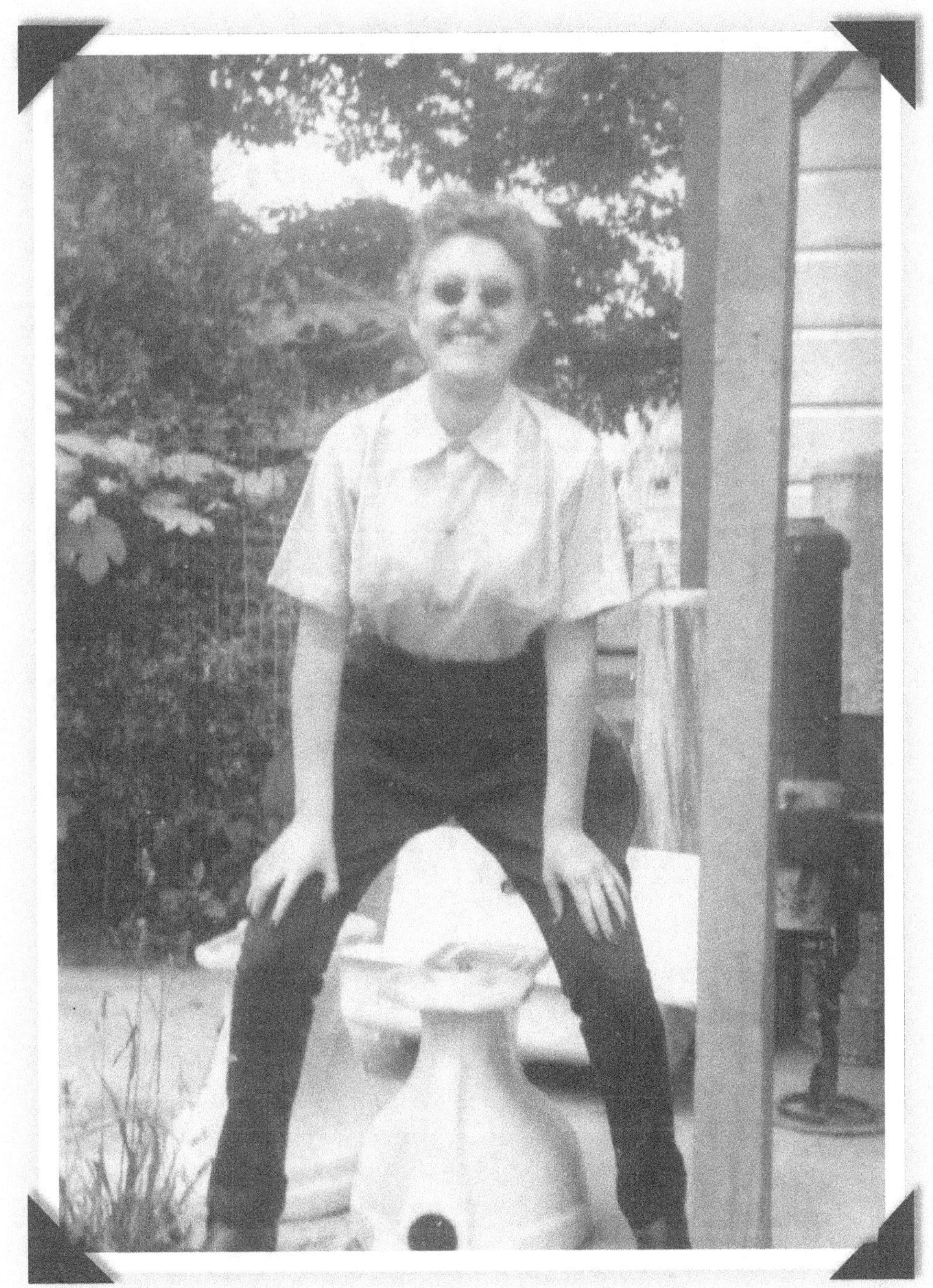

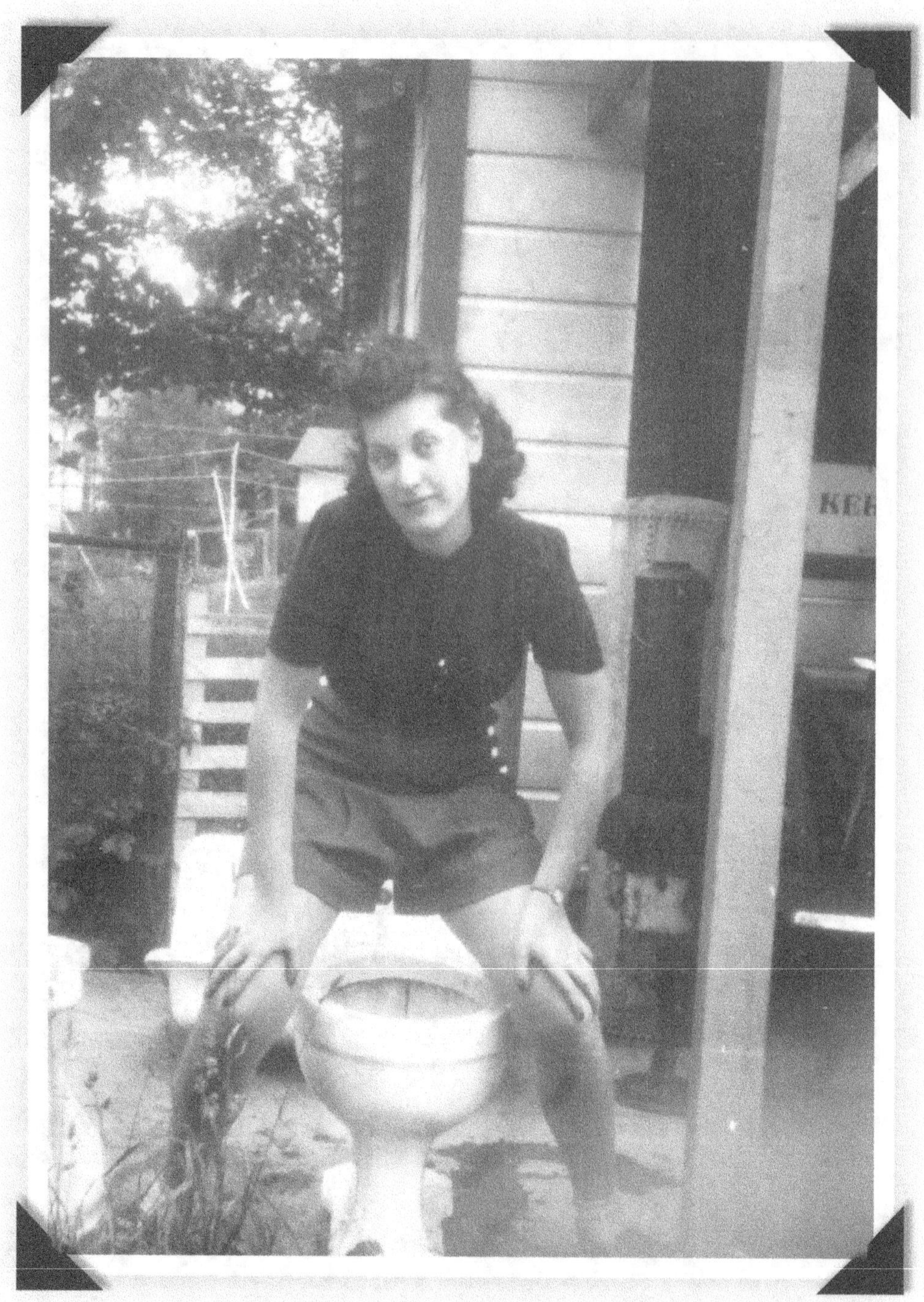

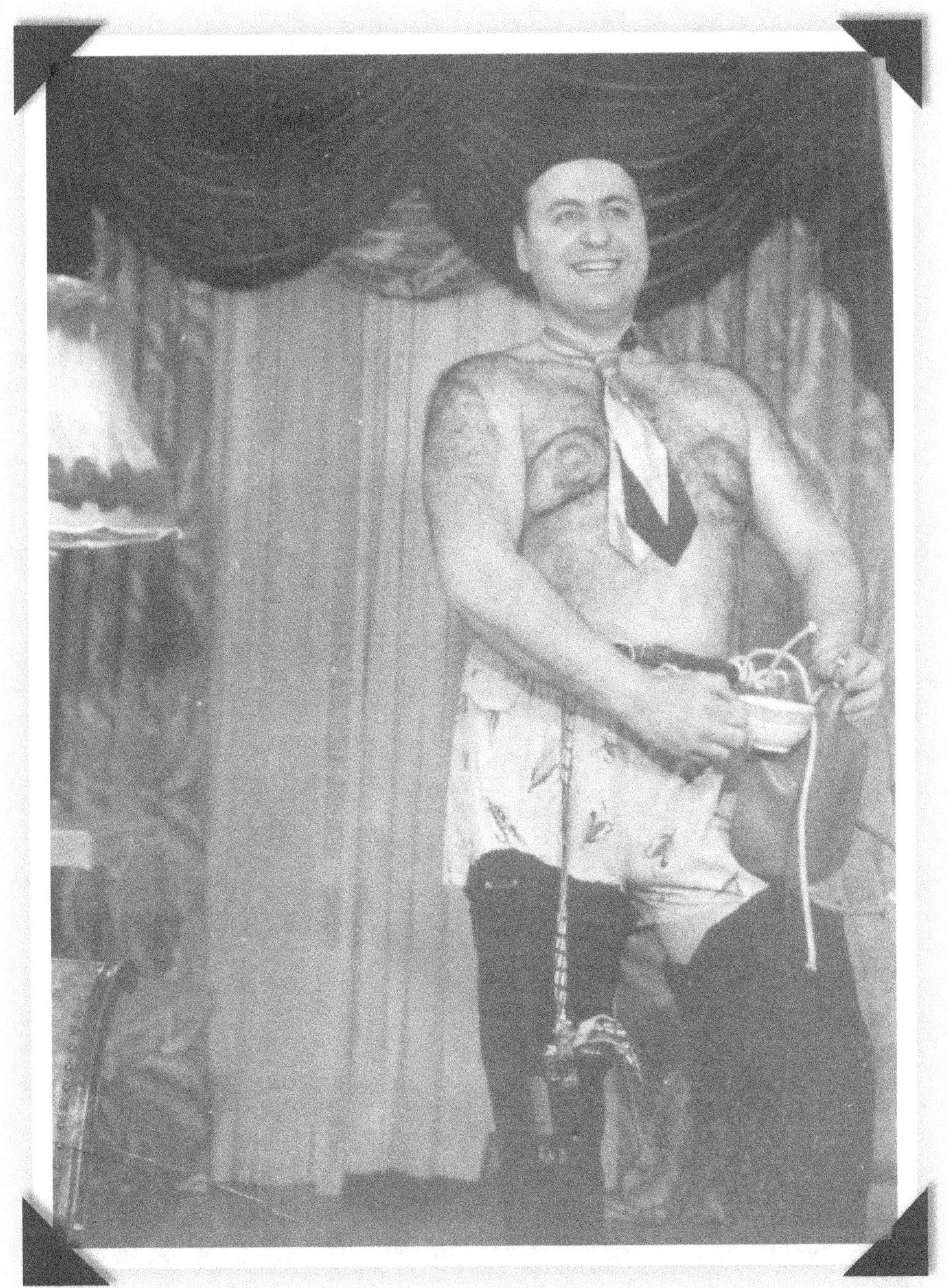

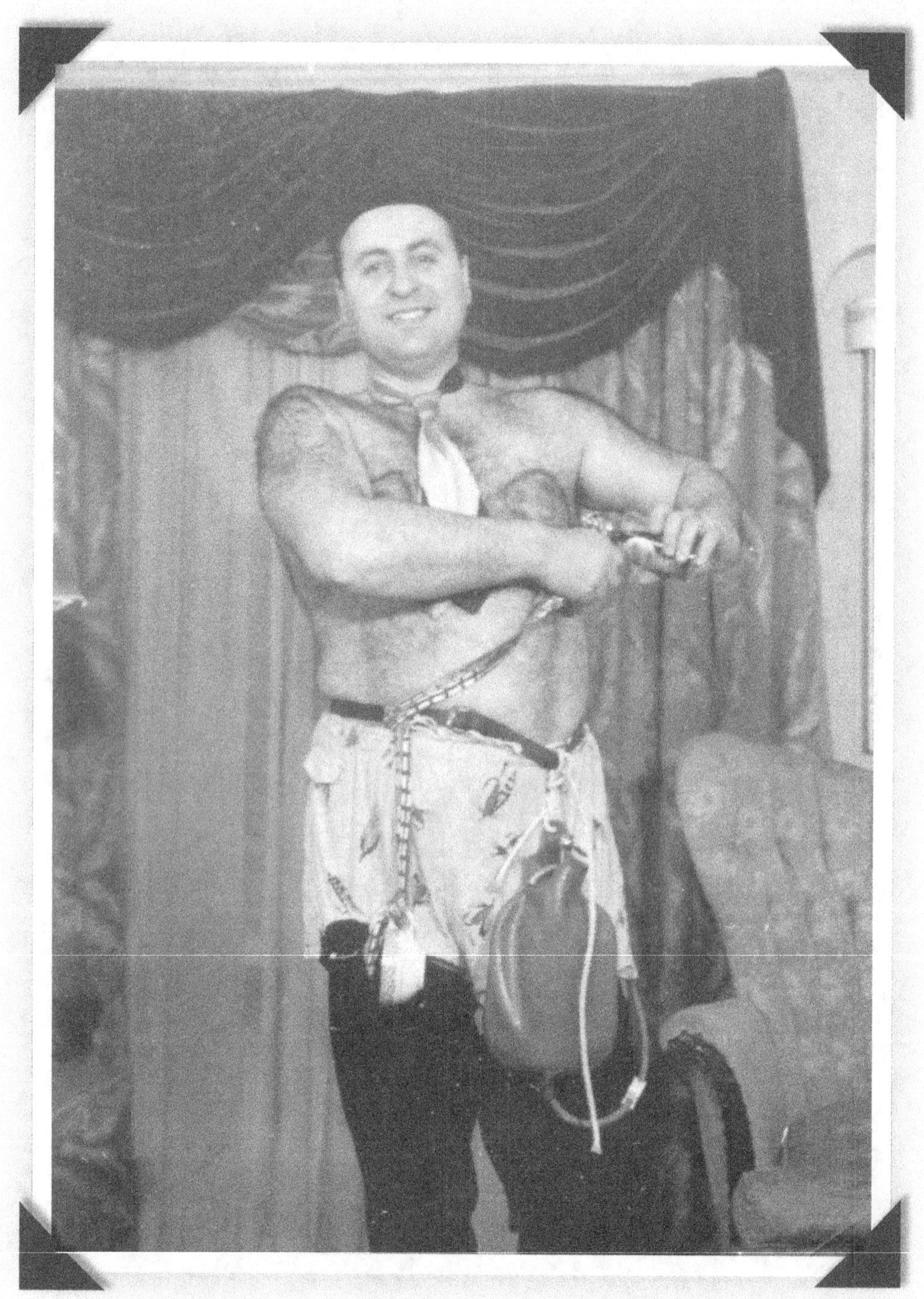

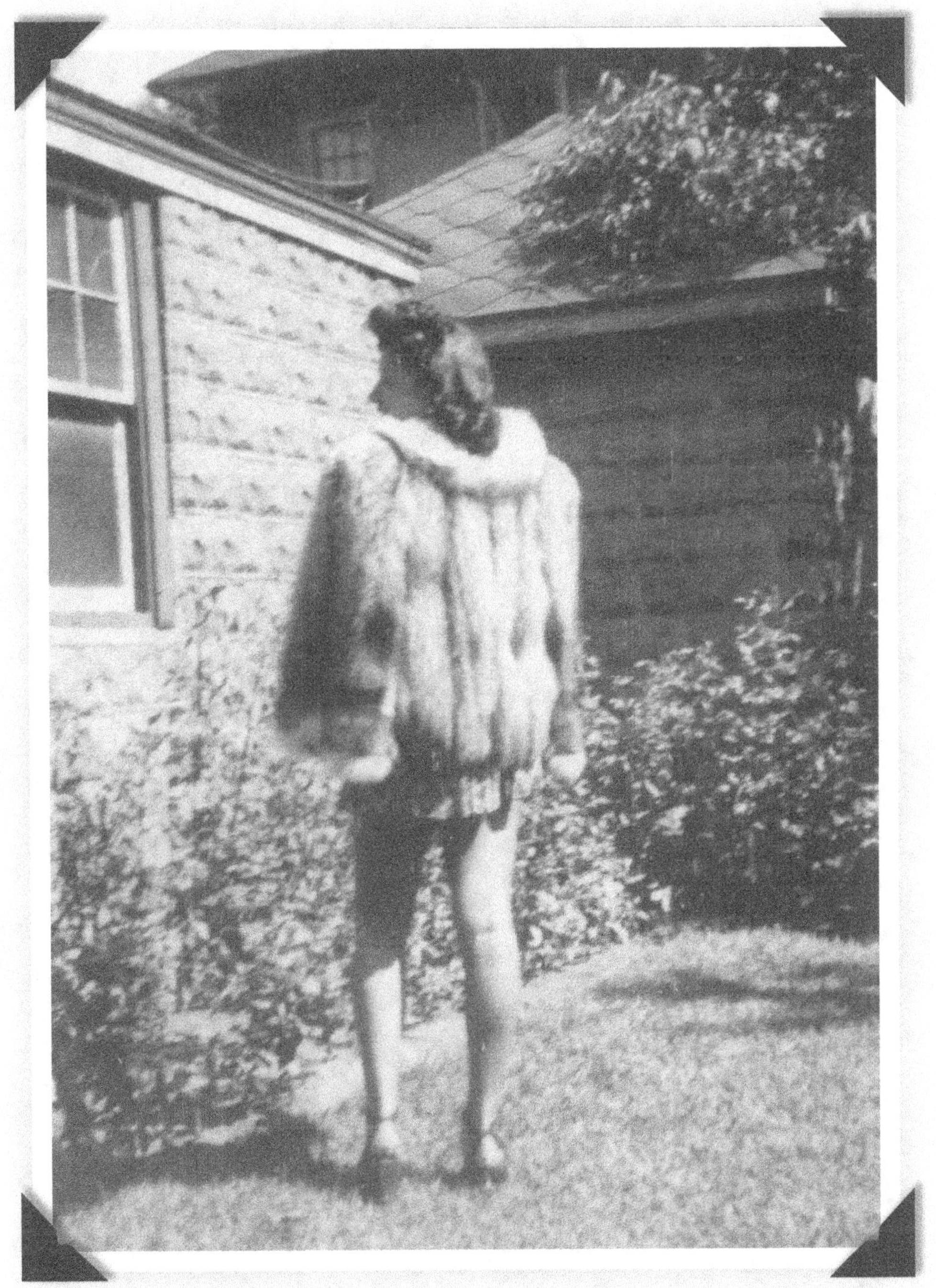

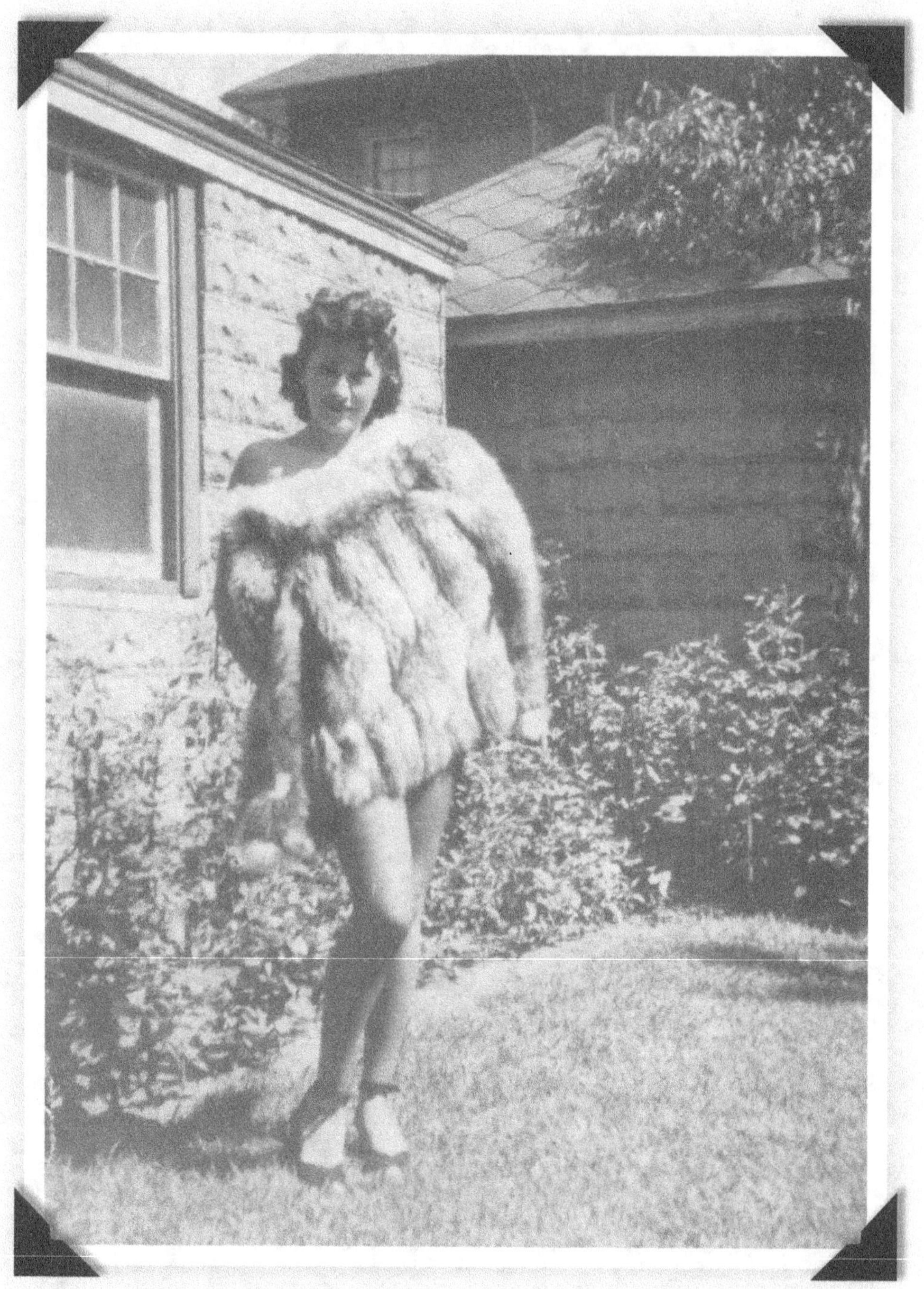

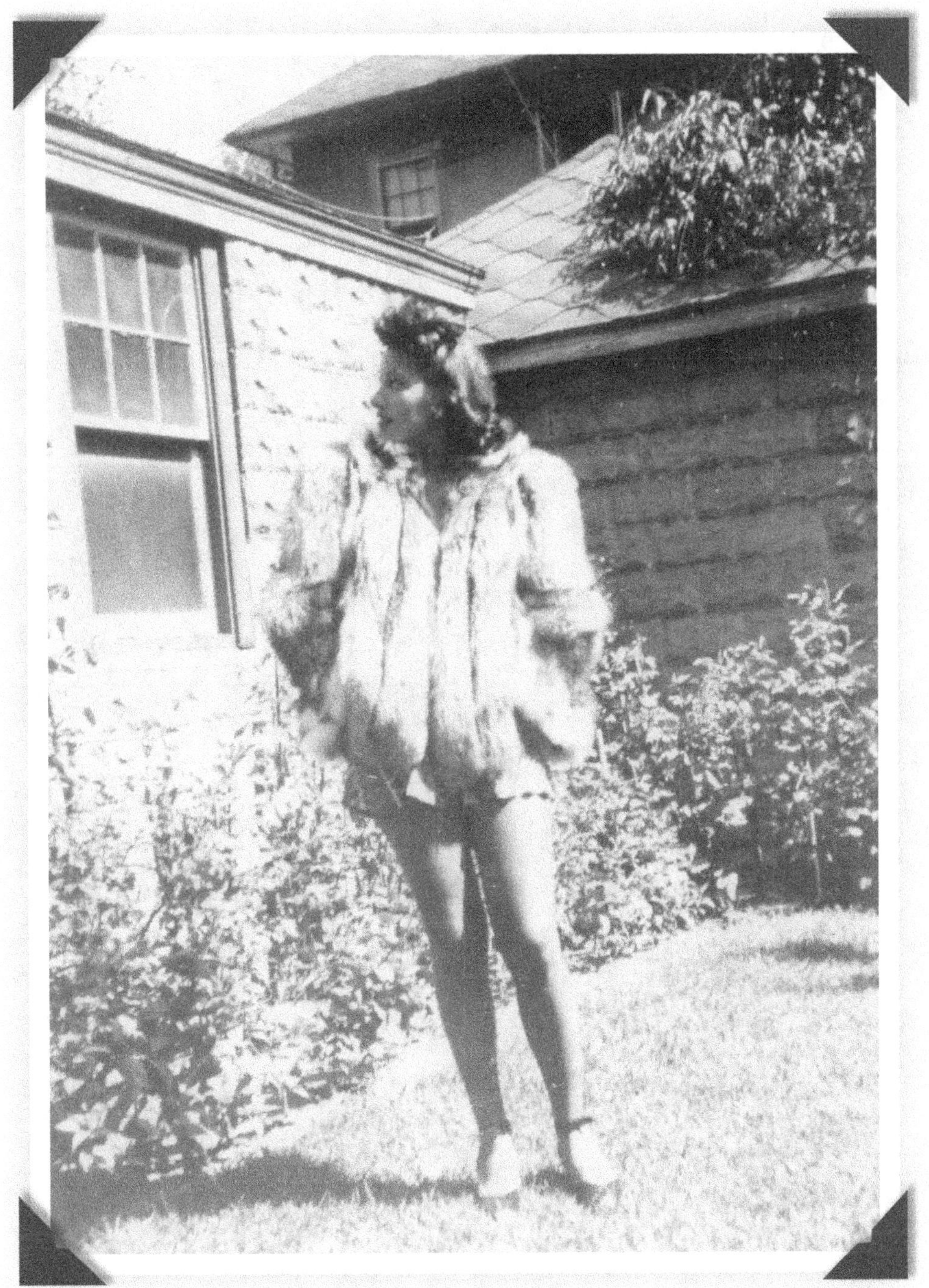

PORTRAITS

In these pictures, I see remarkable and artistic beauty in sweet simplicity:
a boat, a sailor, a bike, a Tydol gas station, and a beach…
are part of preserved images suspended in one defined time.

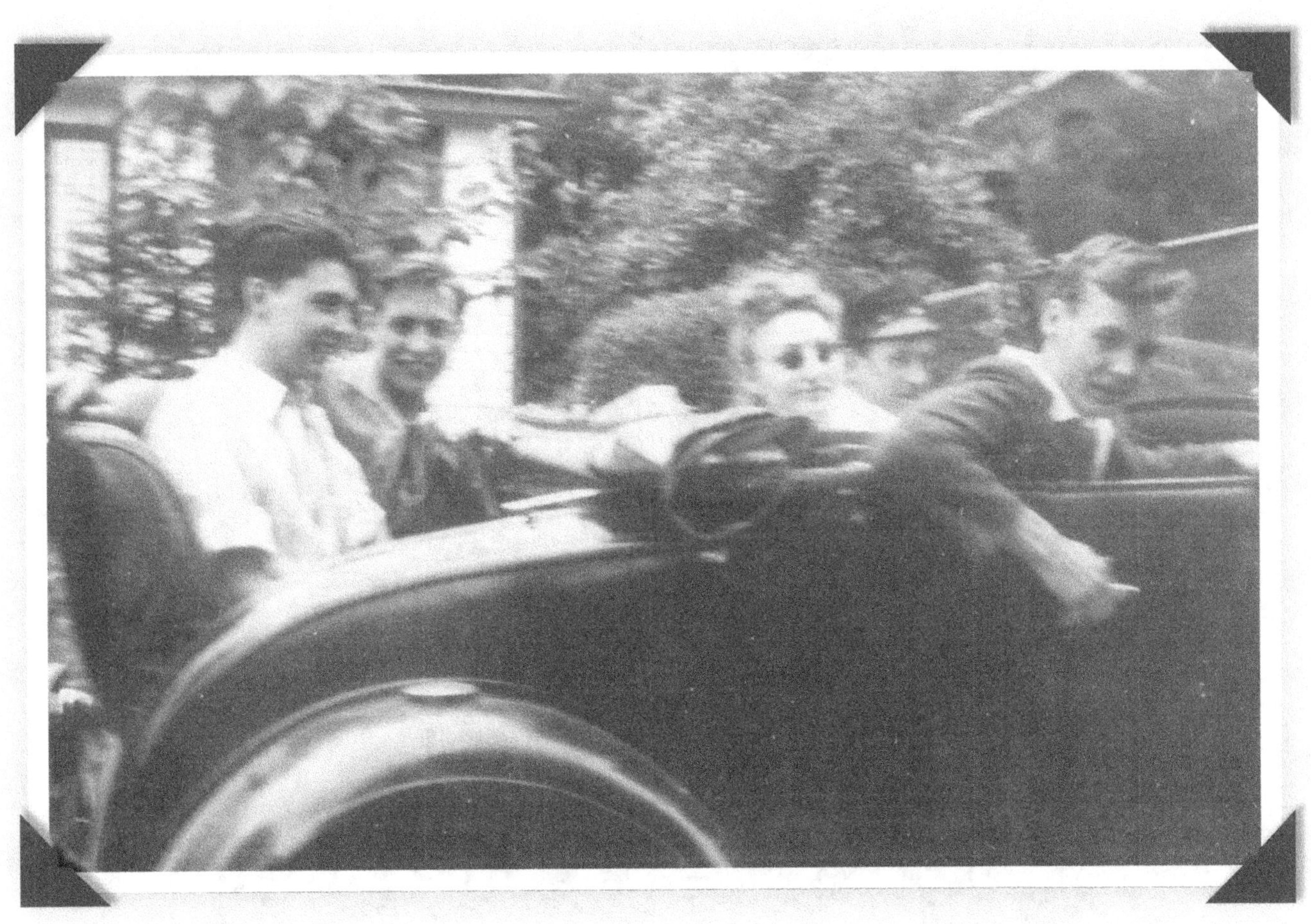

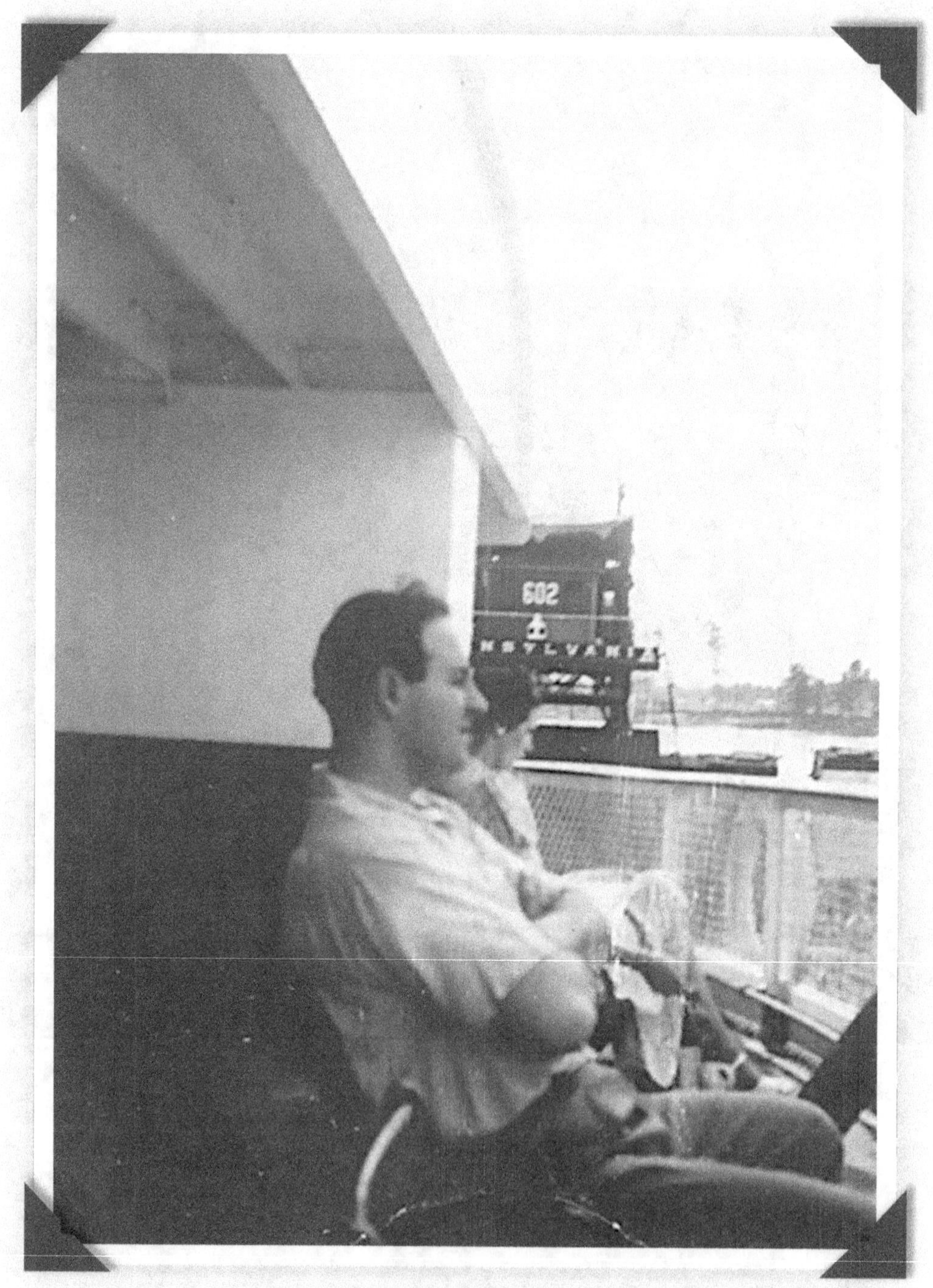

602
PENNSYLVANIA

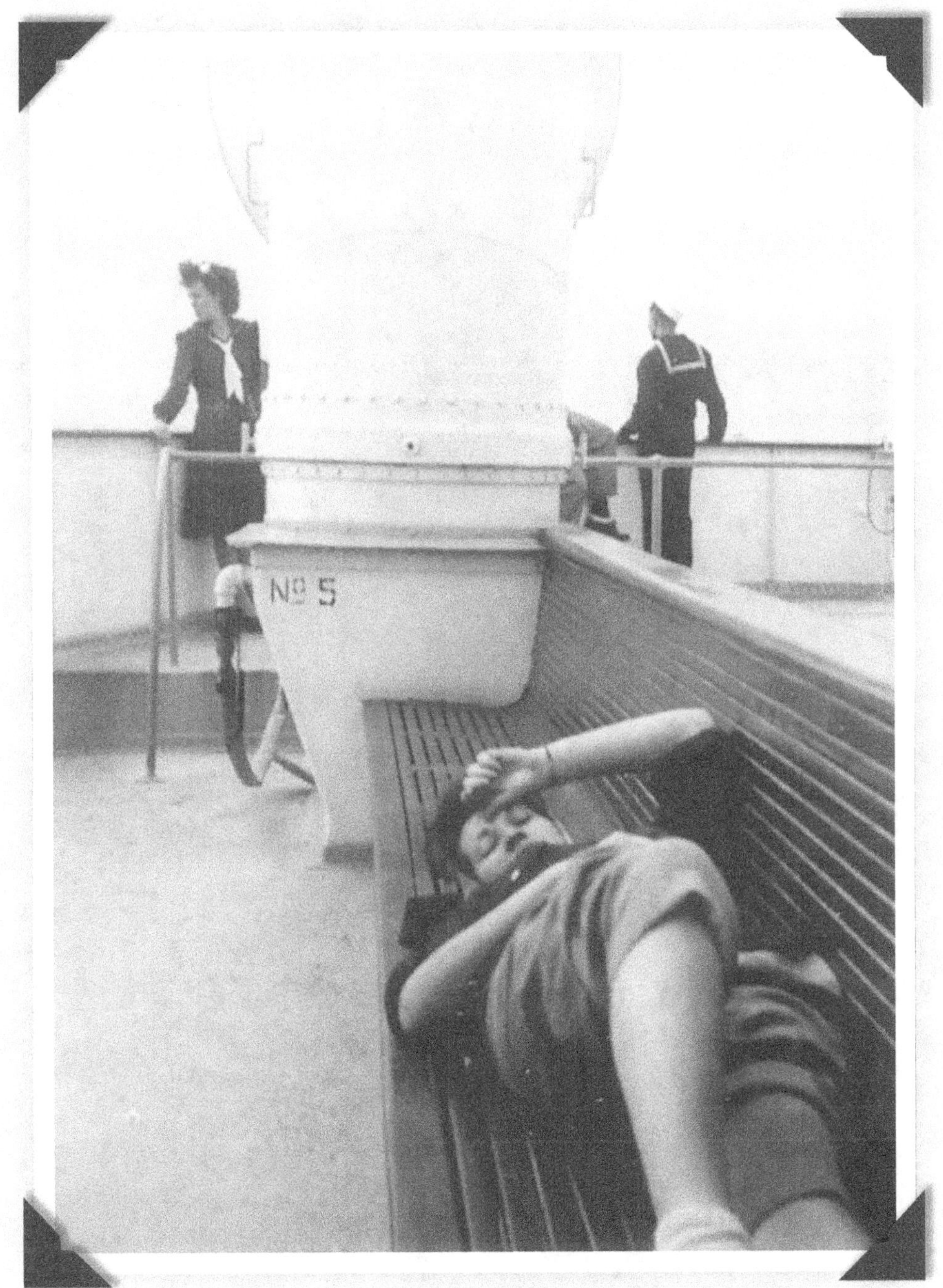

Nº 5

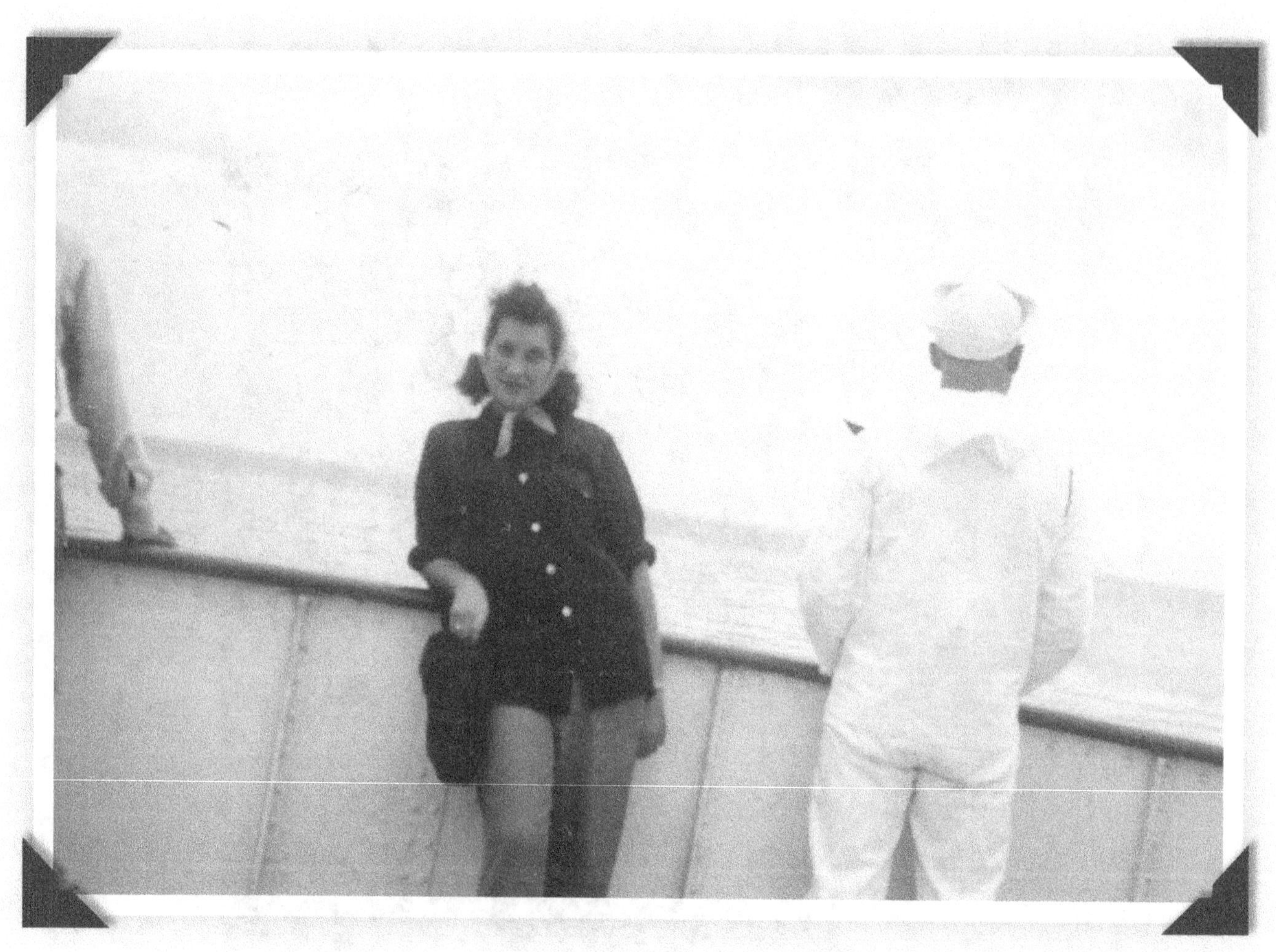

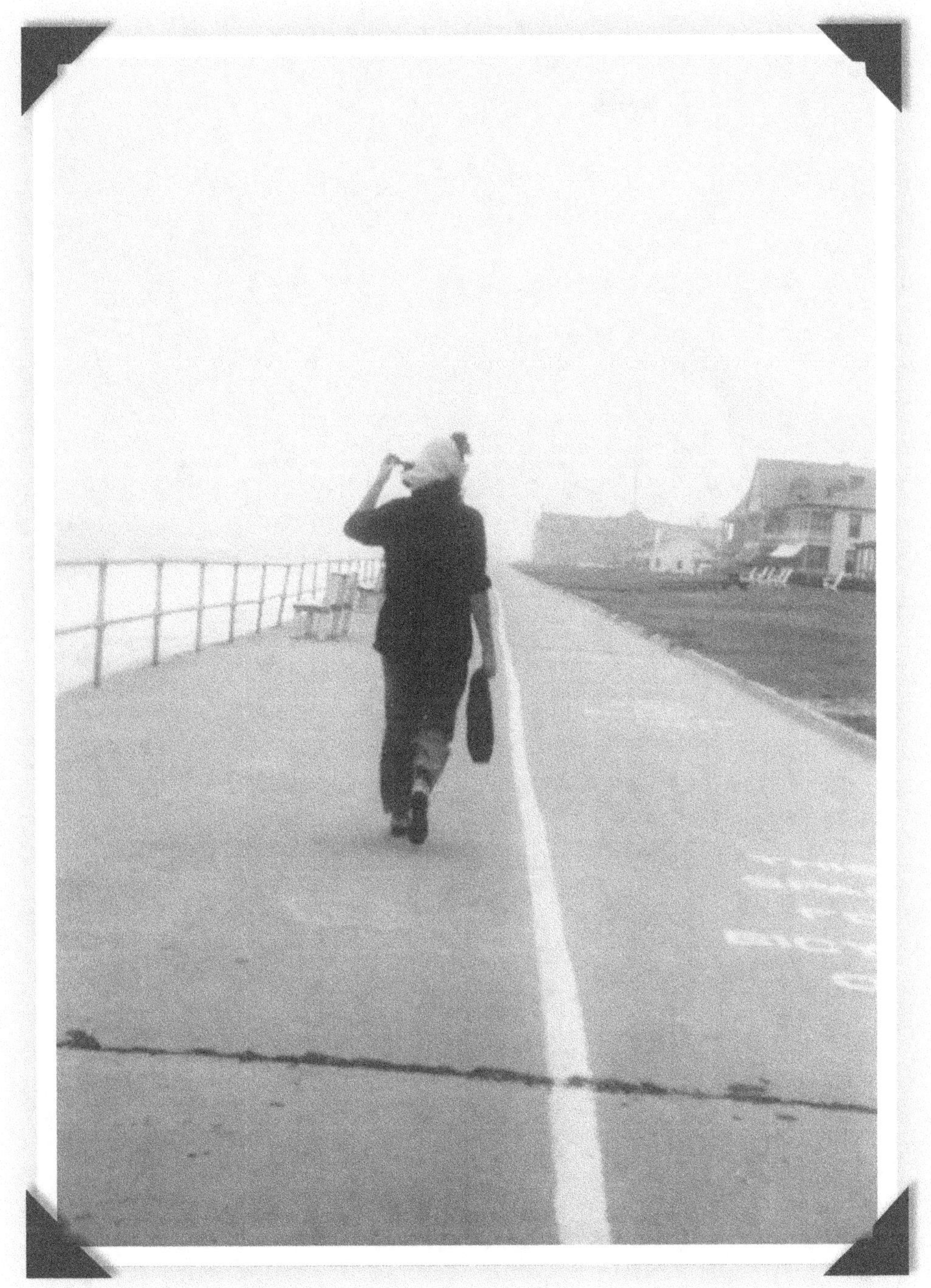

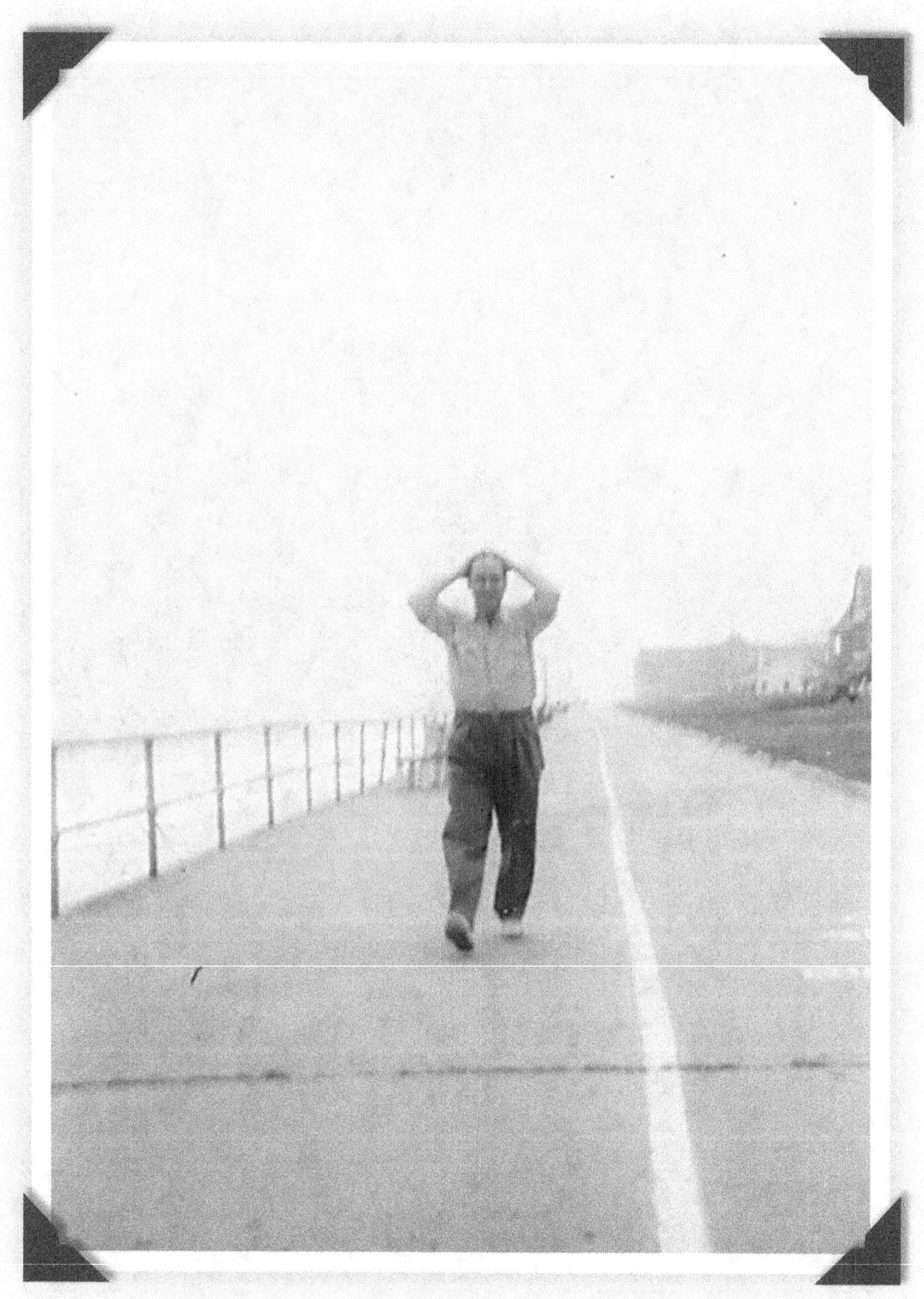

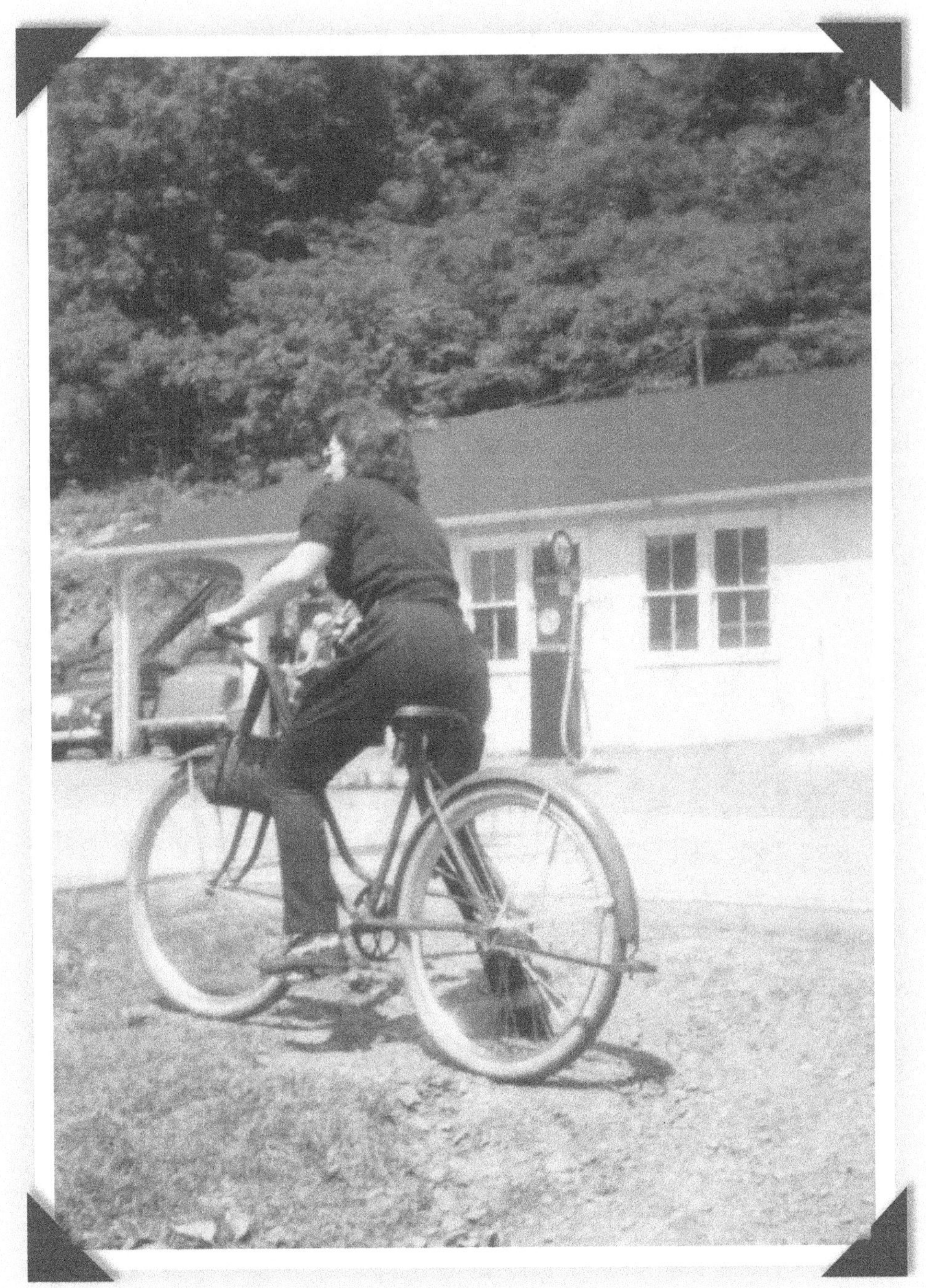

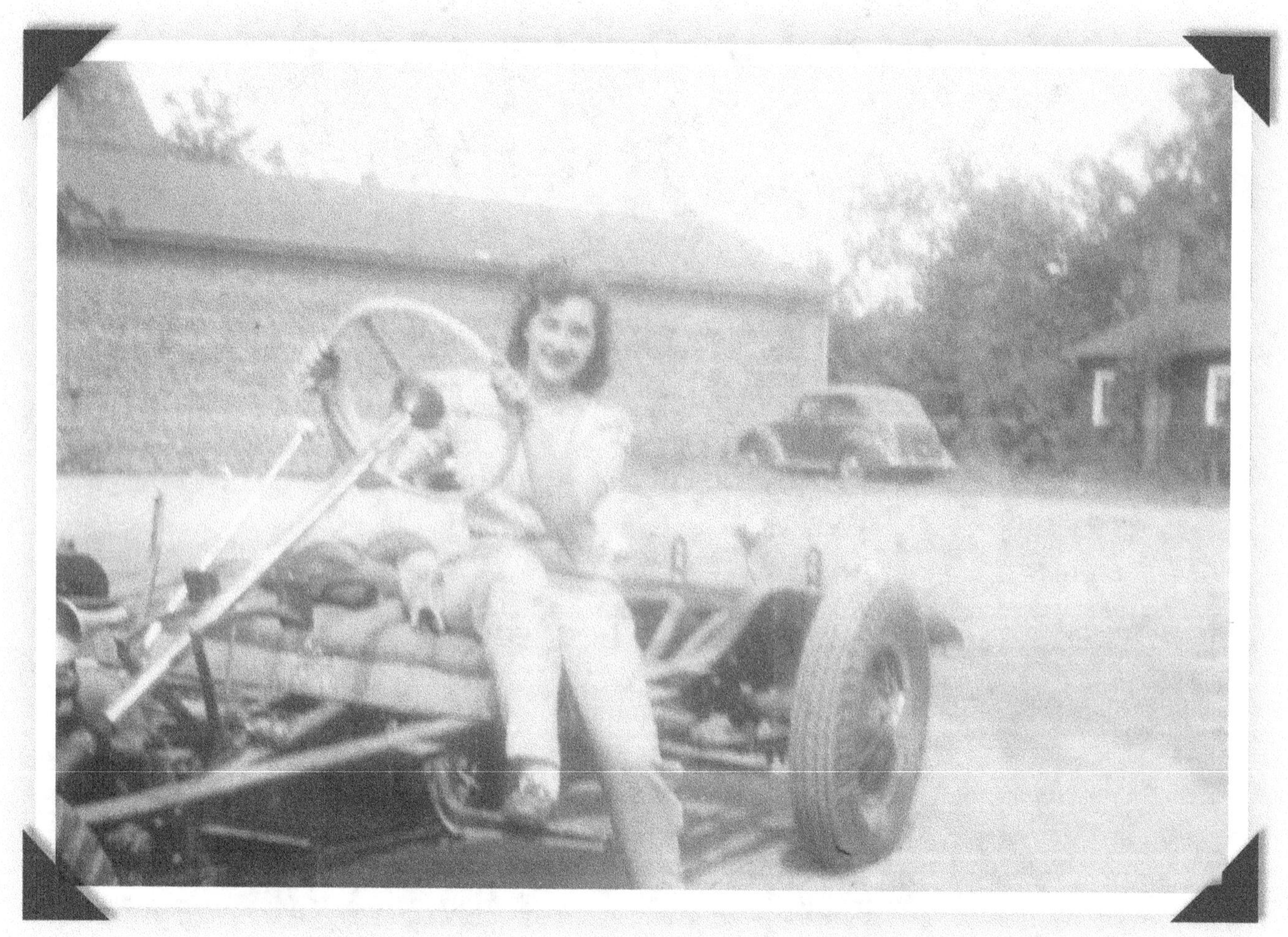

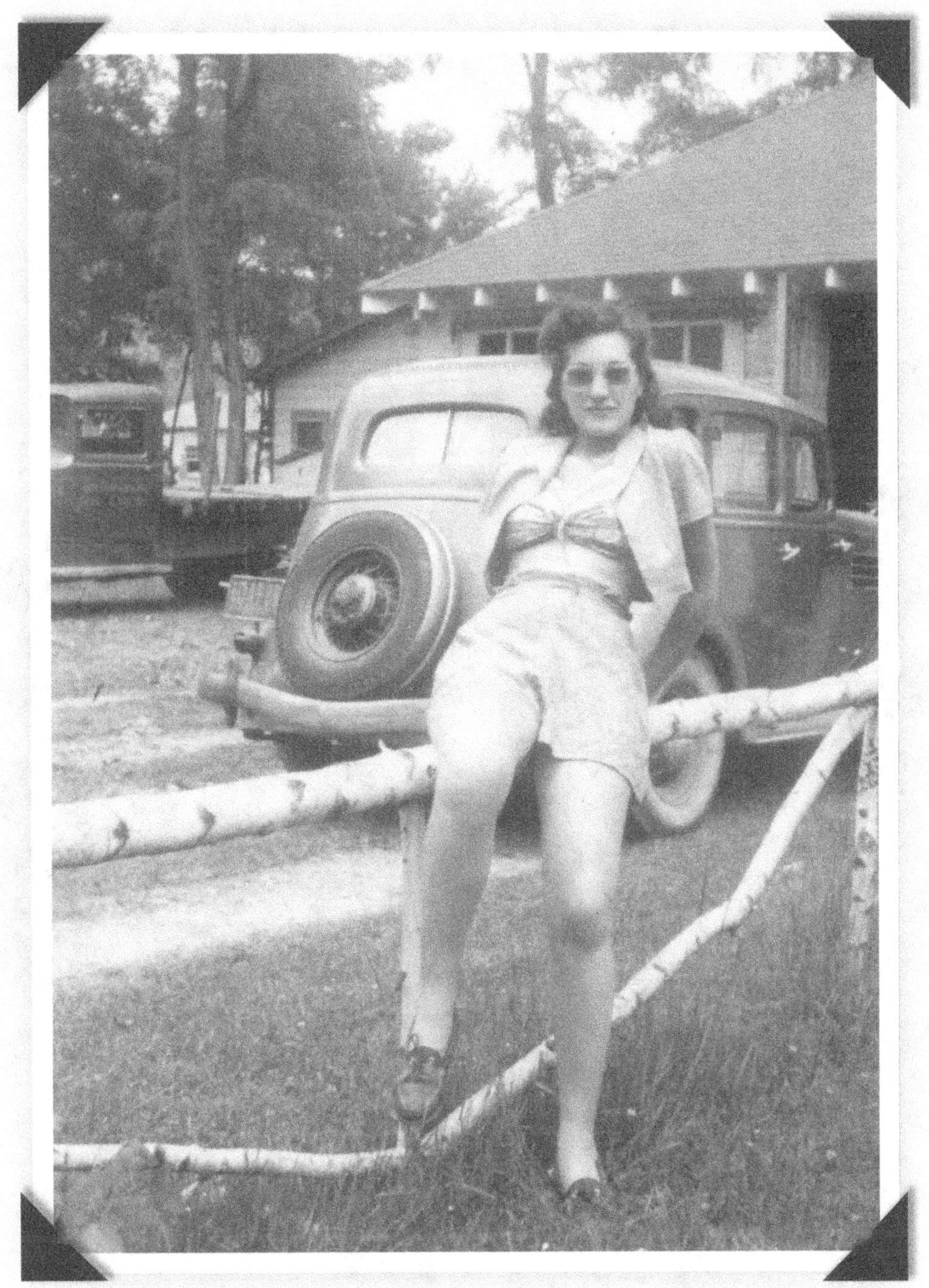

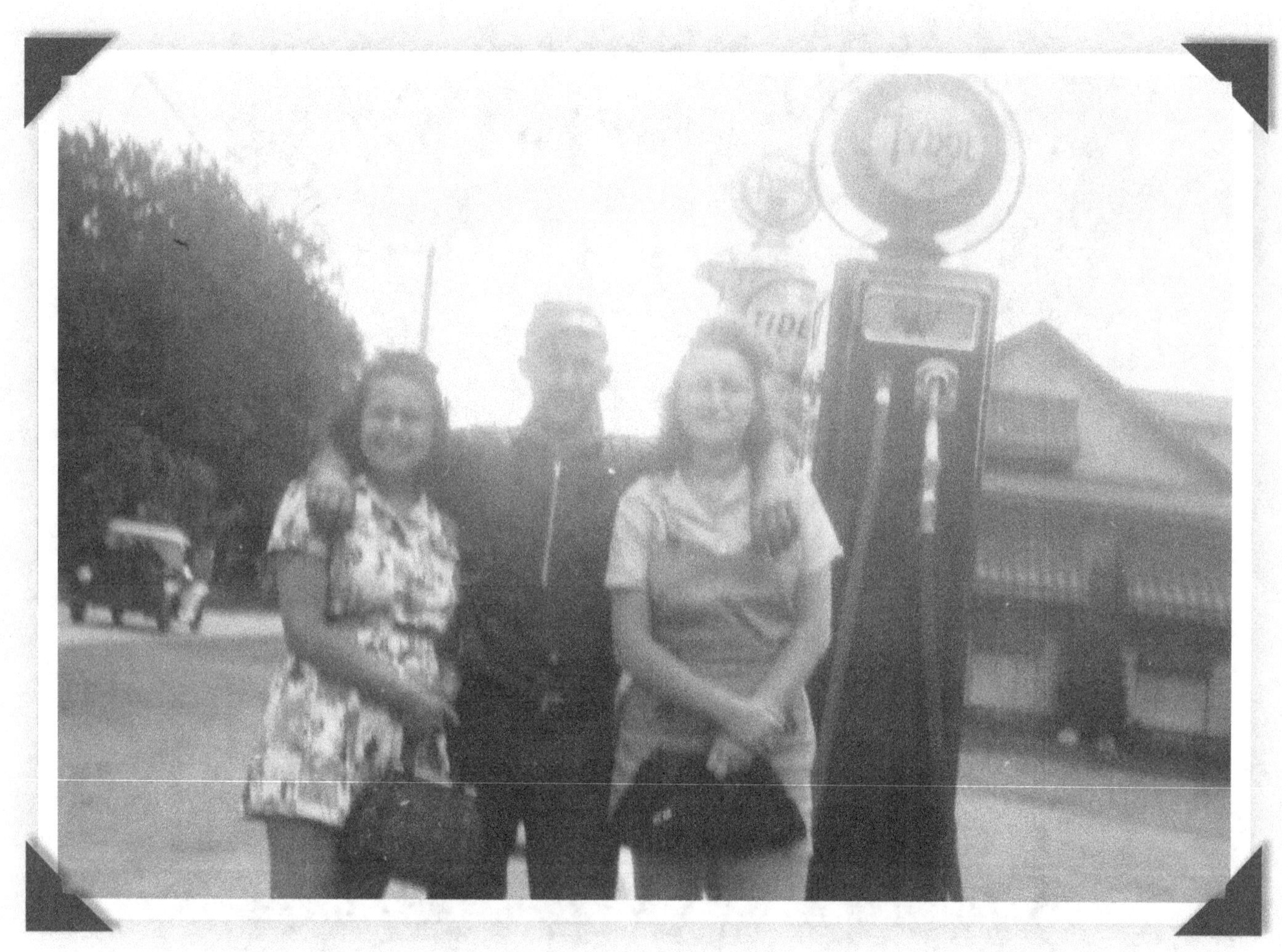

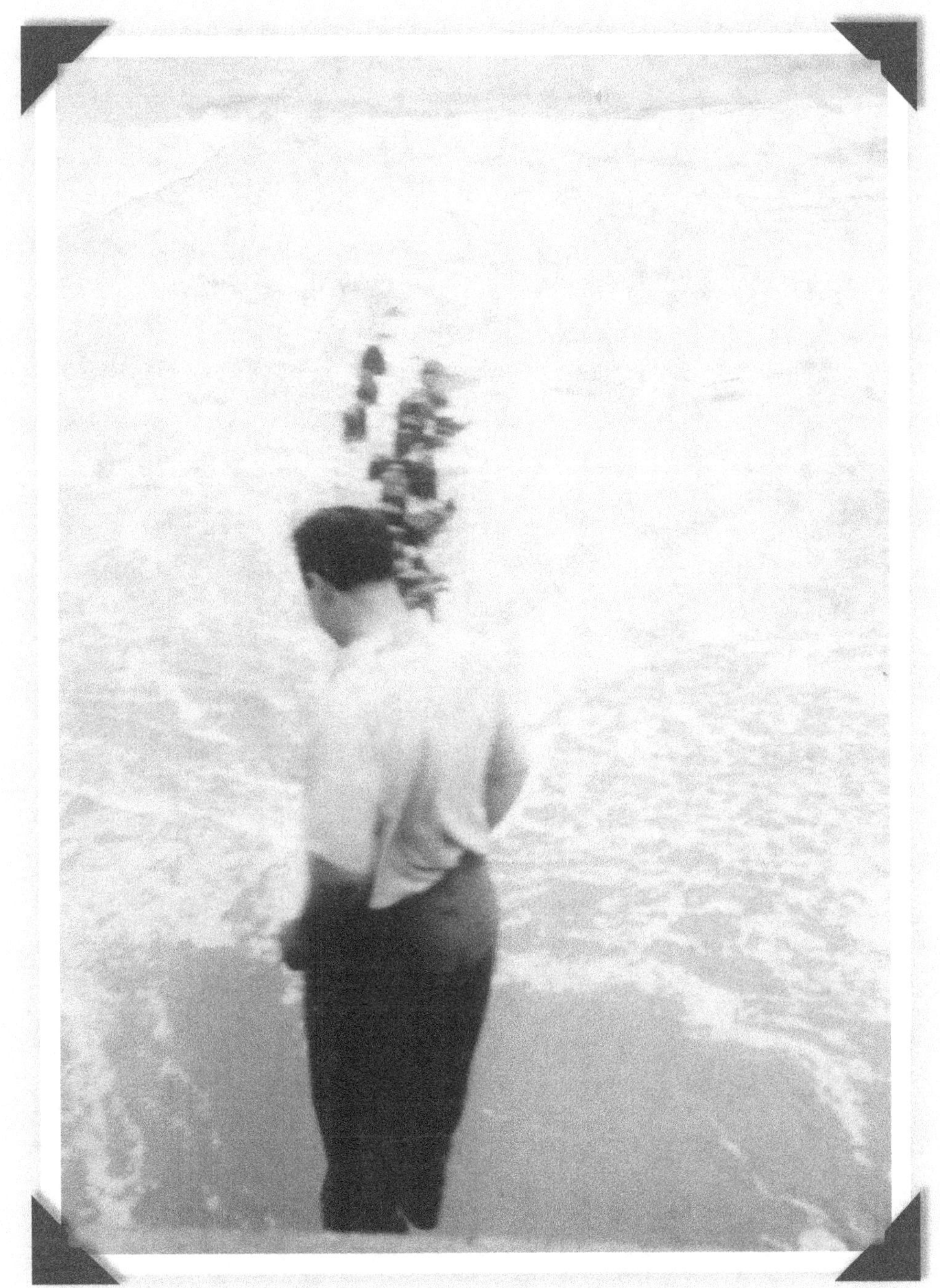

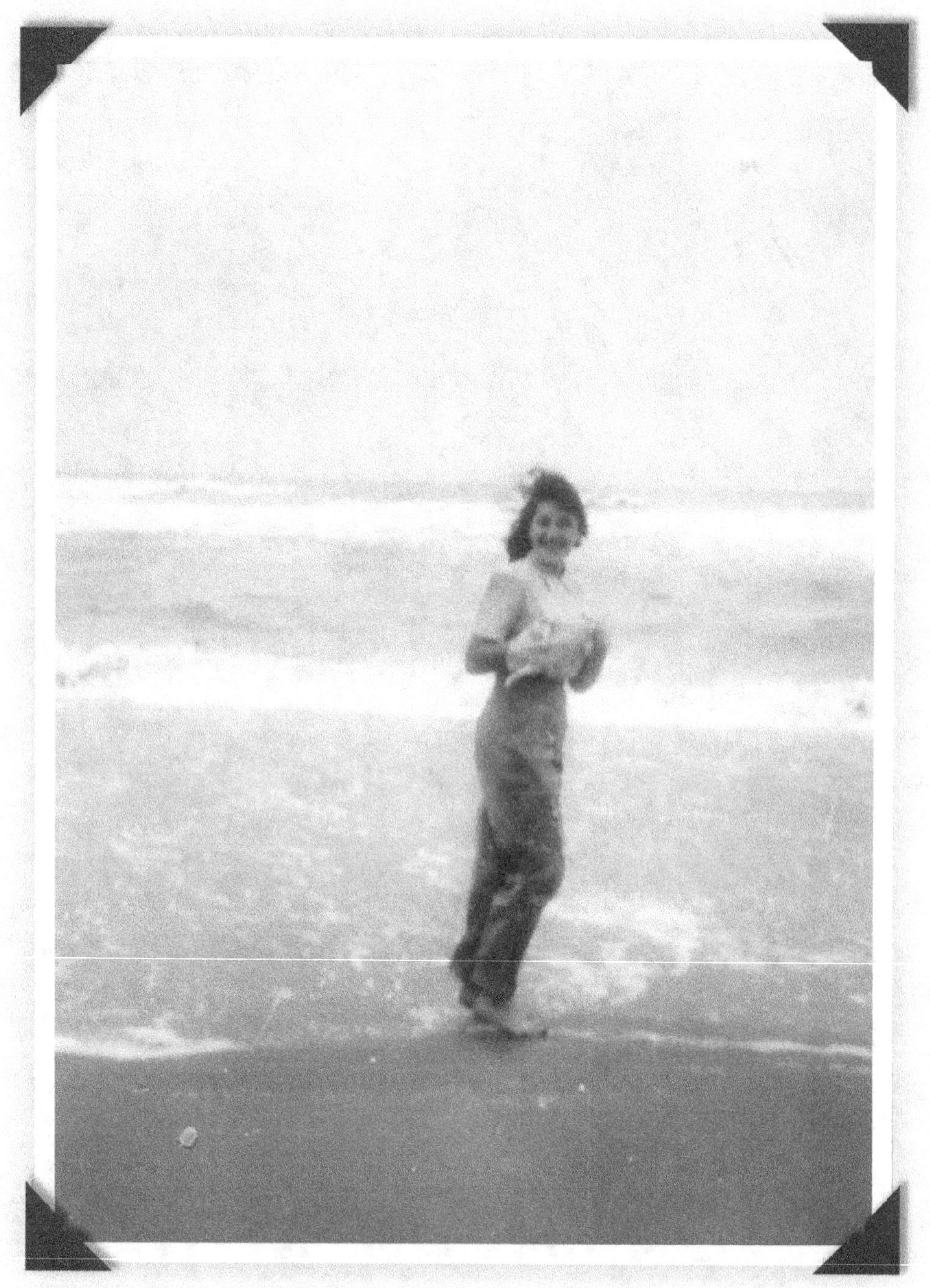

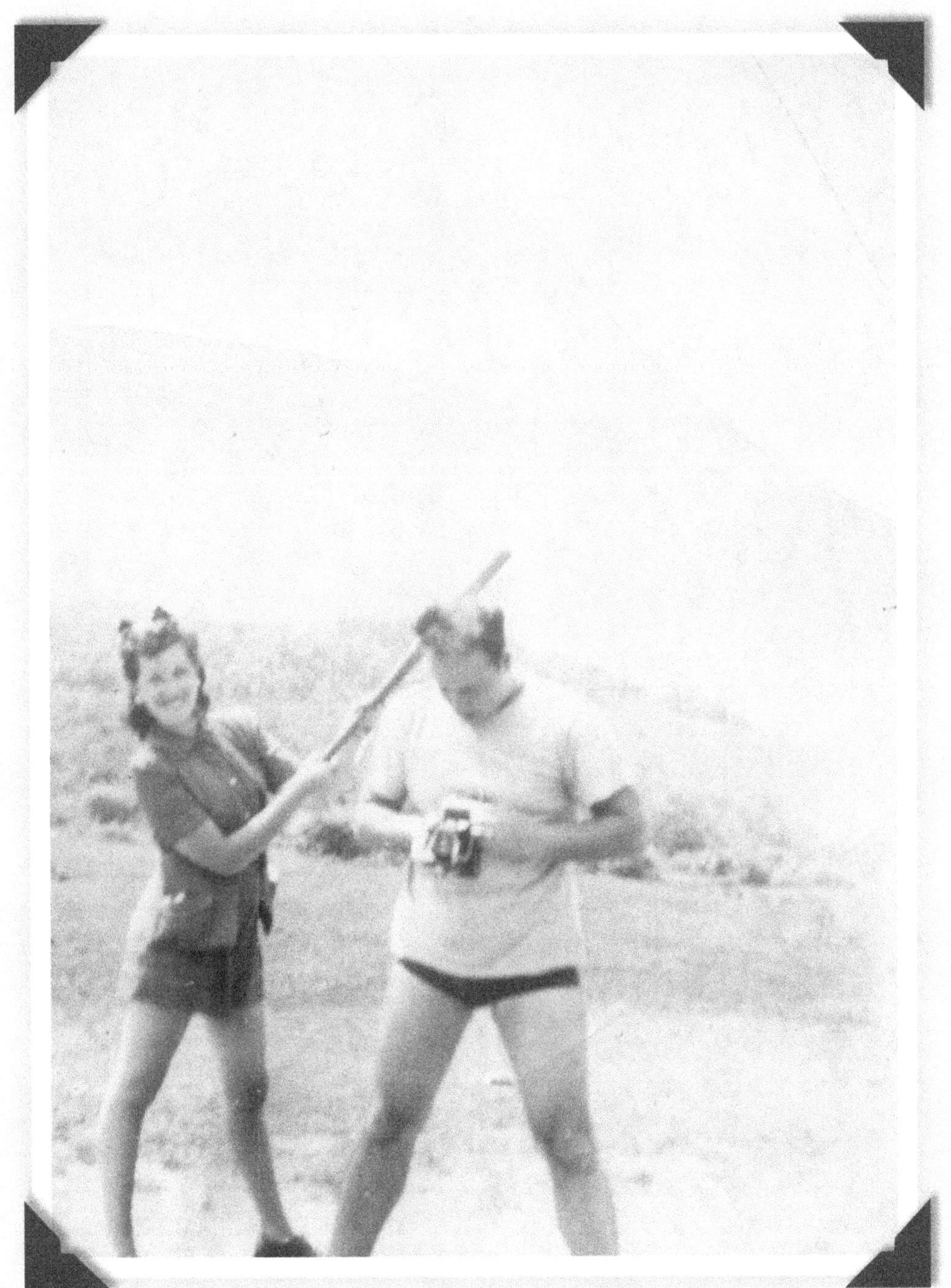

GENEALOGY

It is wonderful to connect to a personal history and see family
I never knew in a very old photo and
to remember relatives in pictures and reminisce about those mentioned
in an old faded letter written almost a century ago.

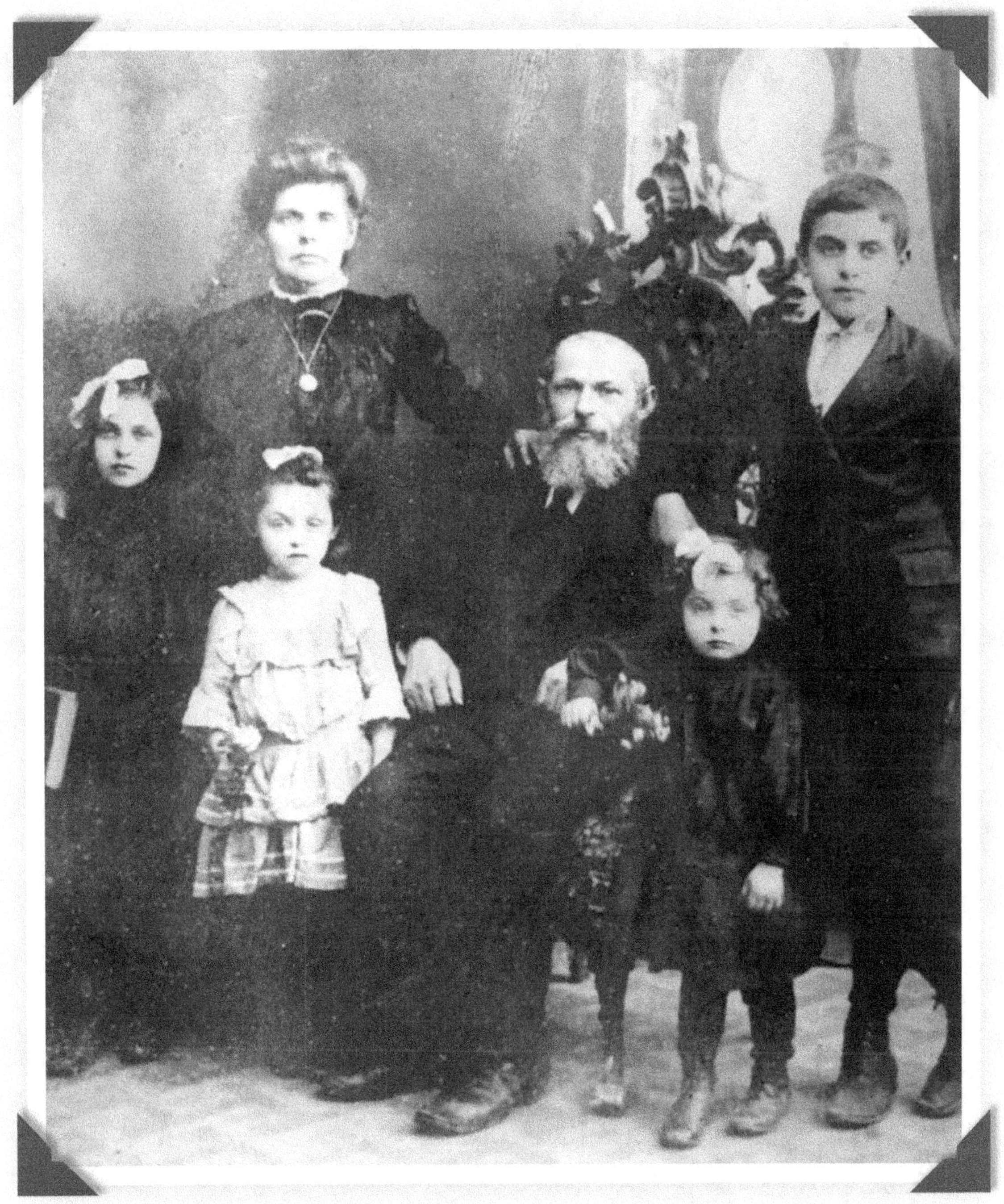

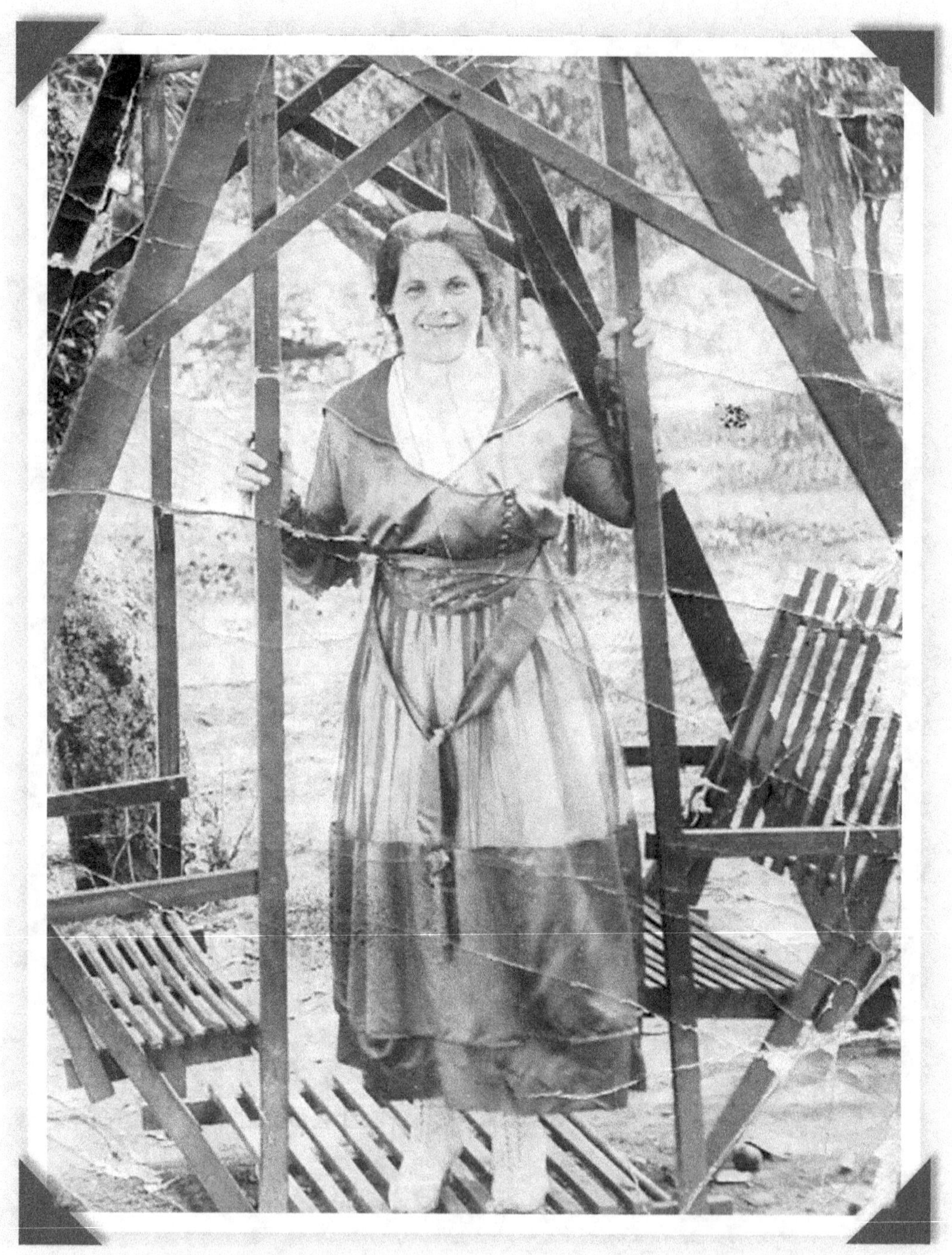

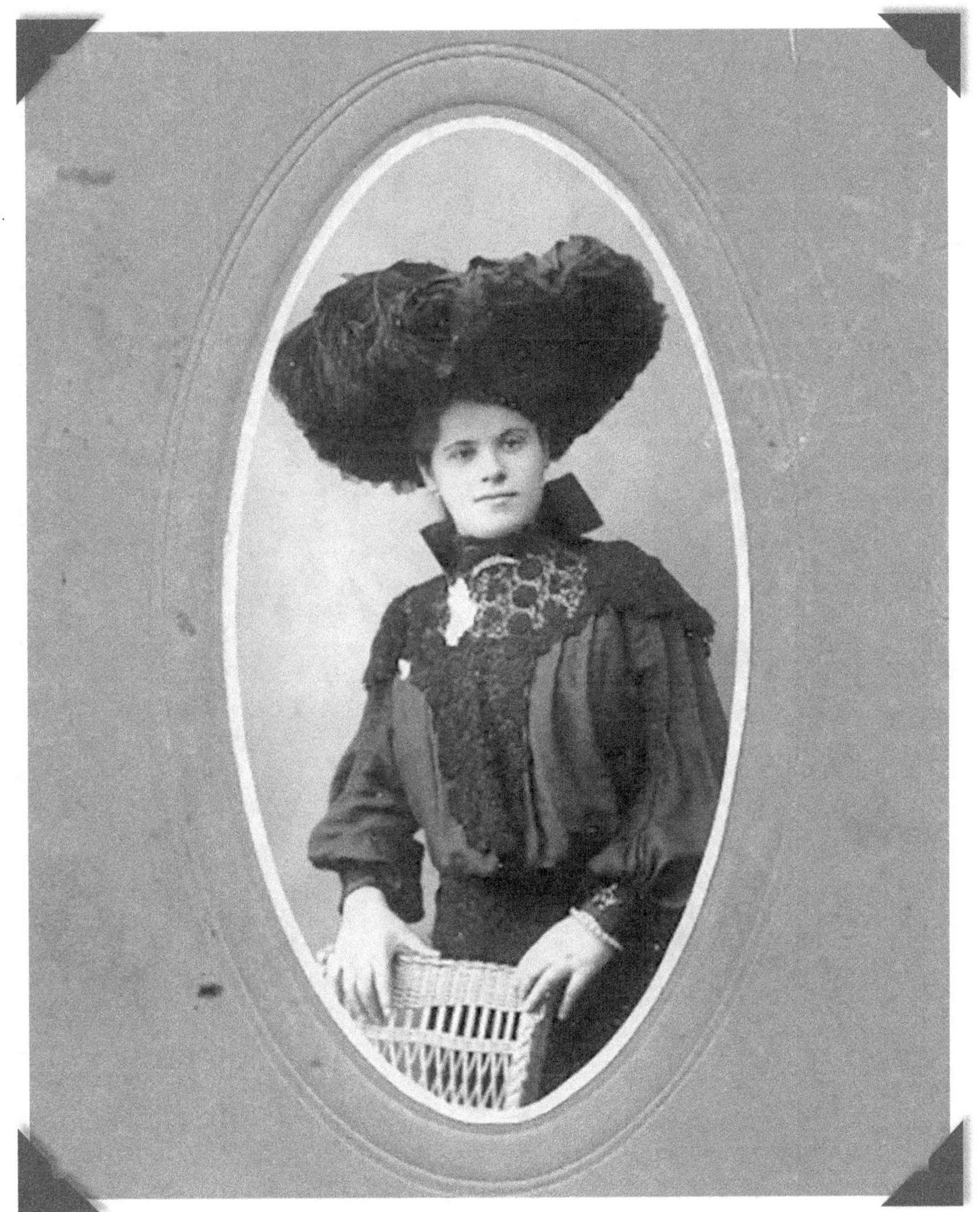

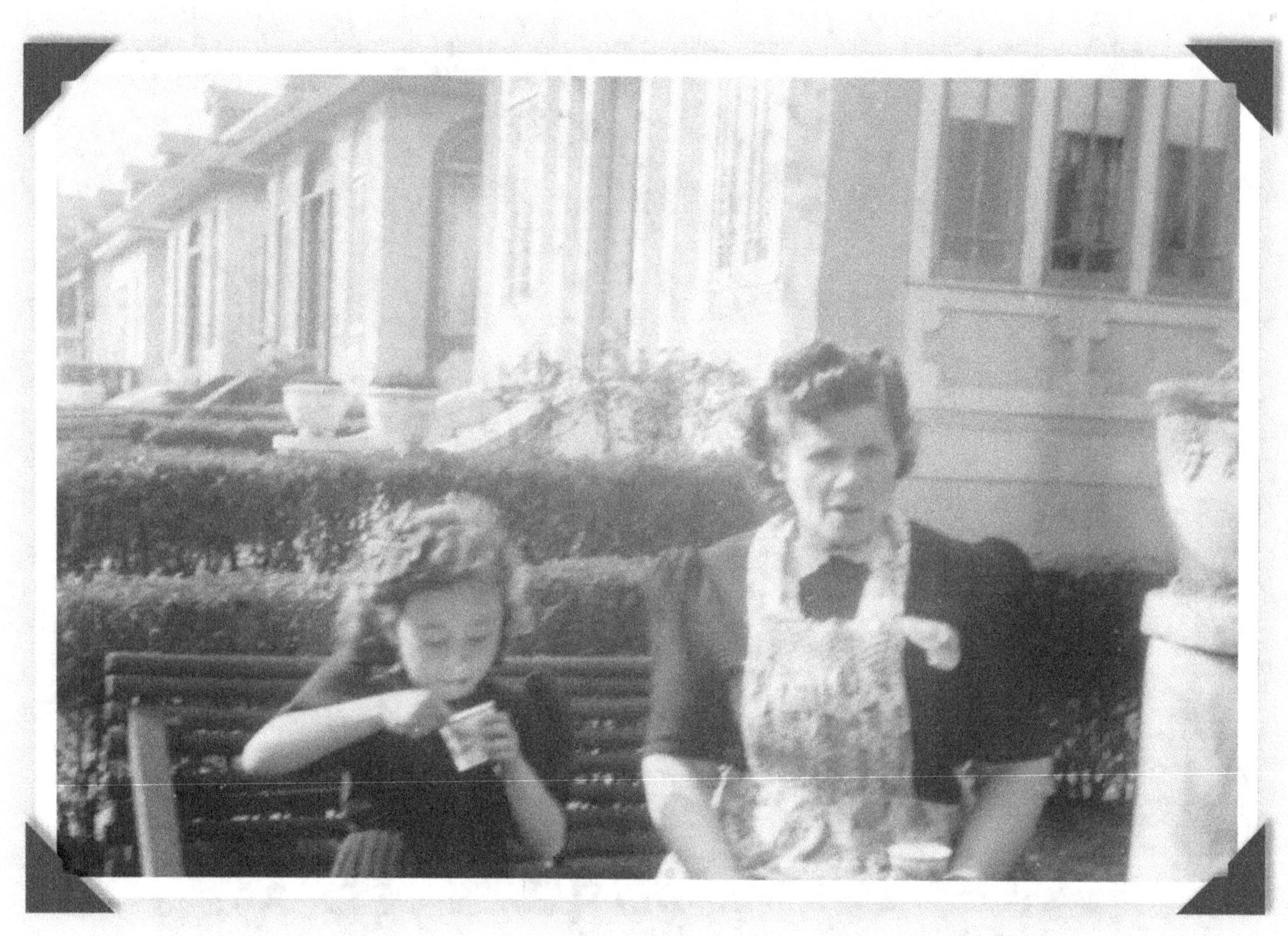

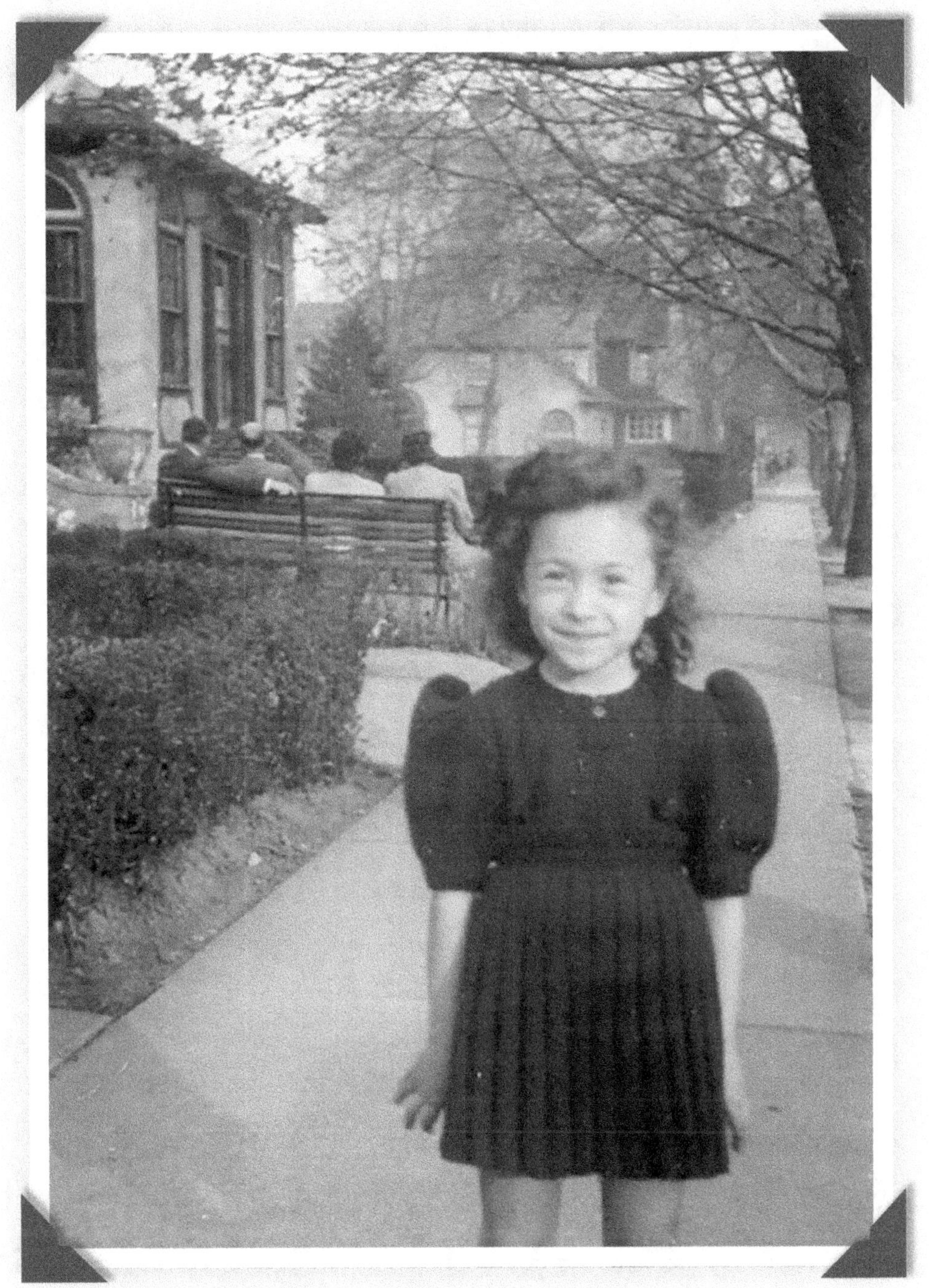

Dear Dorothy

How are you, are you going bathing, with Mrs Kistler to Coney Island, Tell her to keep the [illegible], As soon I get home, We will go bathing.

What do you won't I should get you, how about silk bath robe to match the slipers, What is the matter papa did not call up, he said as soon as get home he call up at eight o'clock,

It is very cold here winter
plenty of snow on the ground
that you sleigh ride & ice skate.
And Charlie if he wants a police
dog three weeks old; his
cousin would get me one free
very good one. If Aunt or
Basil calls _ I would be come
home _ _ How is Robie
know is he still fighting with
you. And he any different
_ I am away tell him
he should eat meat go out
doors for his health go out
for a ride every night
that he will sleep well.
        Best _ good to all.
            From your loving
                mother

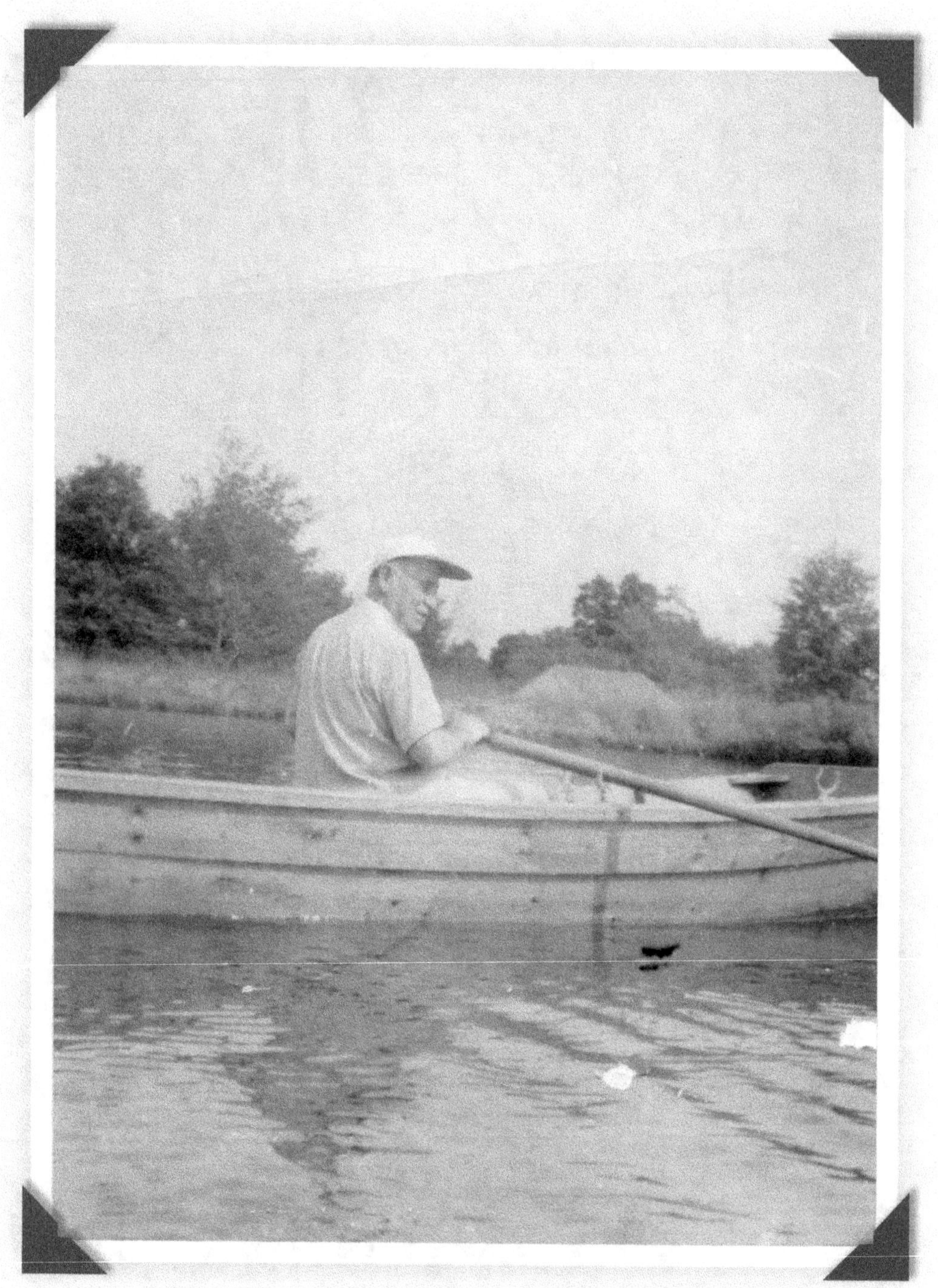

QUANTUM LEAPS

Time passes and so much becomes grounded within the previous decades:
a nap under a tree, old cars, cold snow, unknown stark landscapes
and Coney Island… define lifetimes.

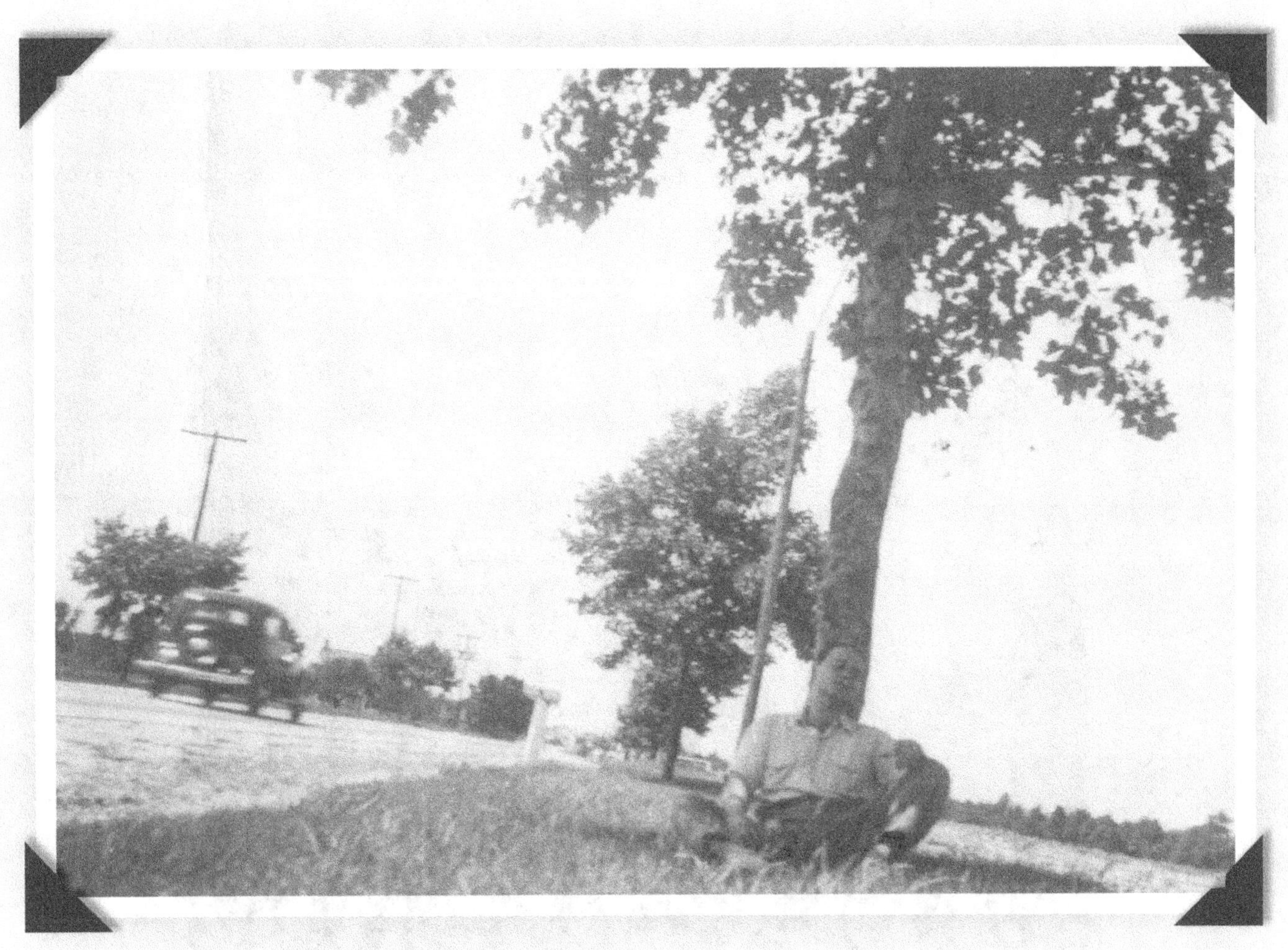

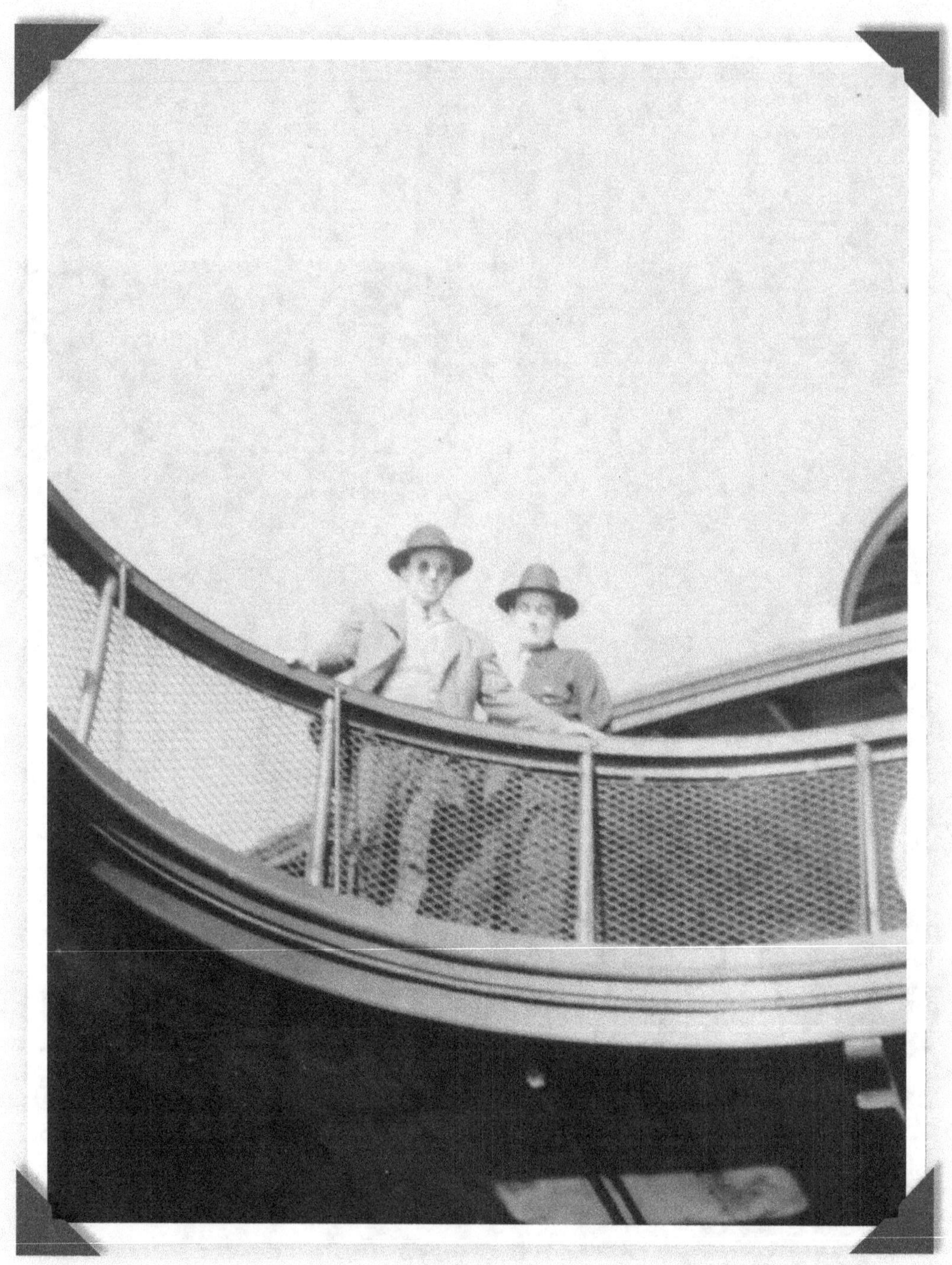

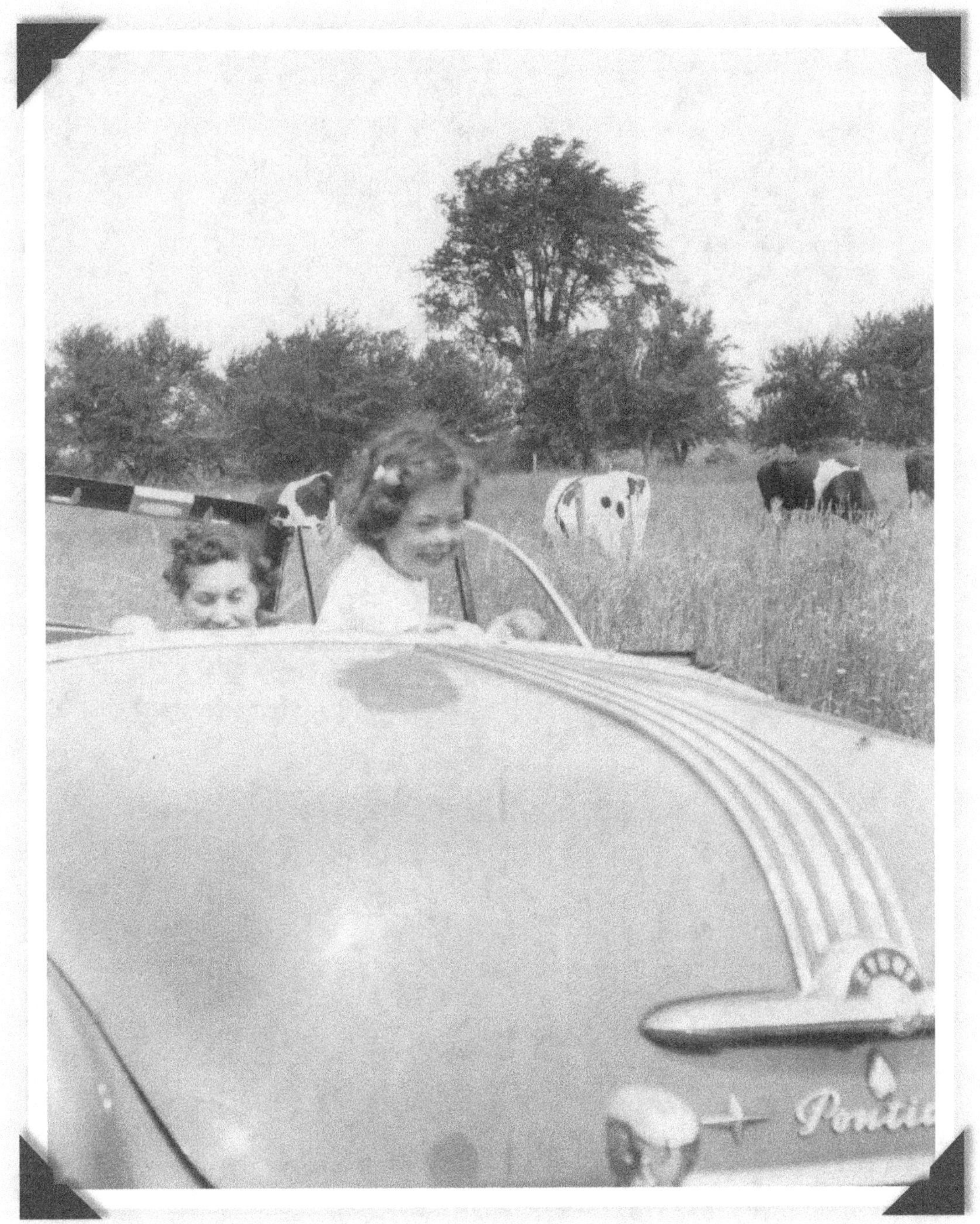
Pontiac

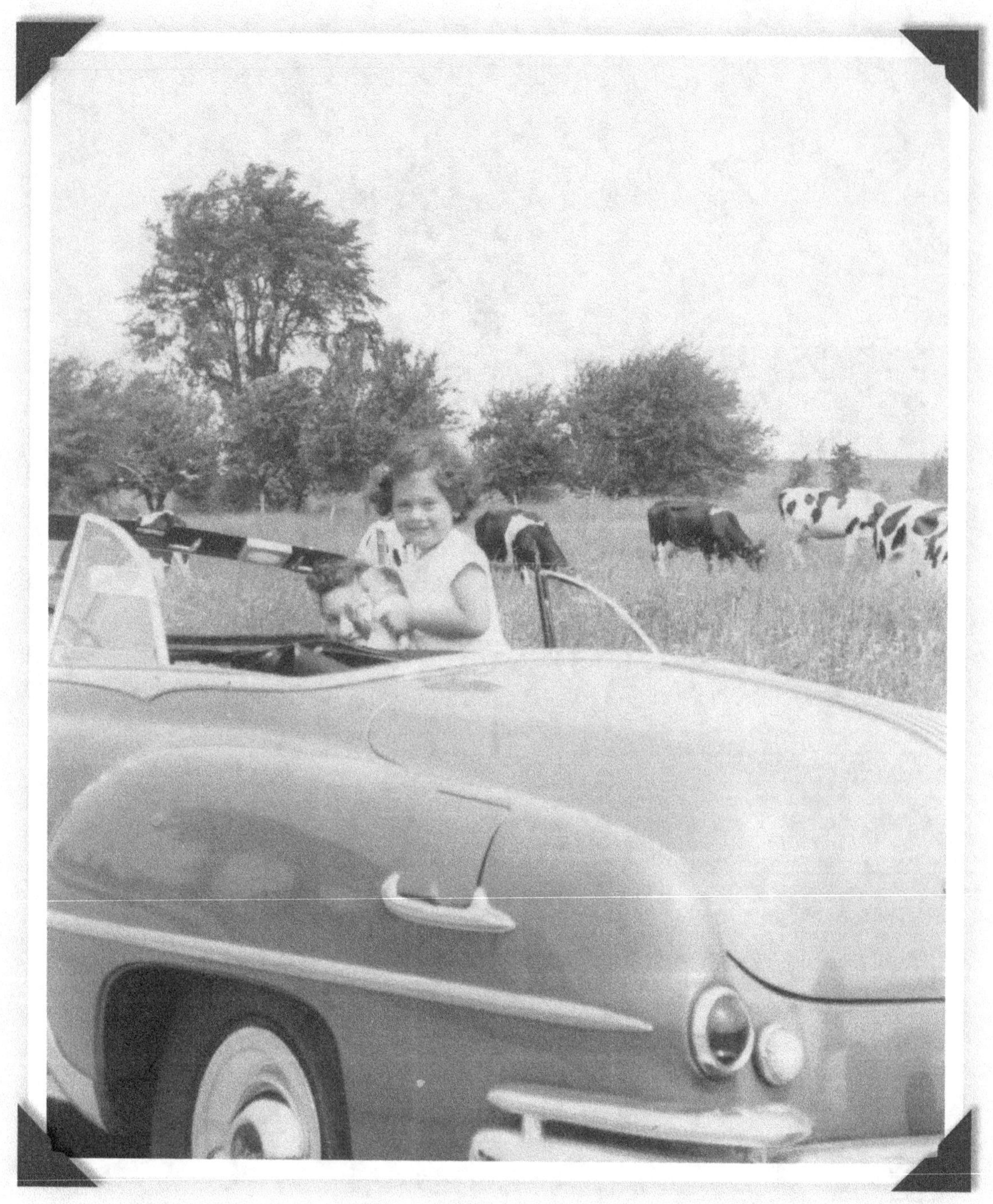

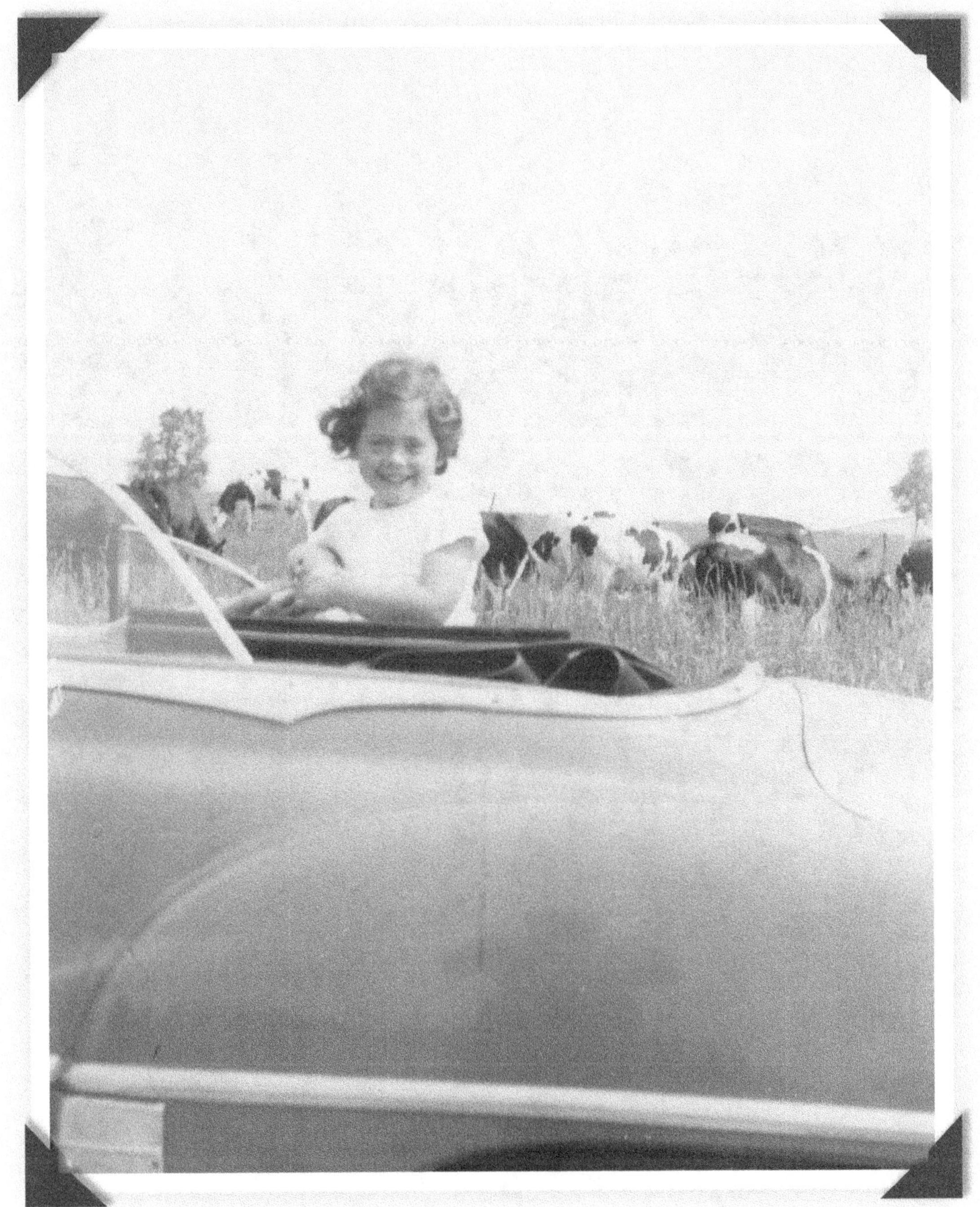

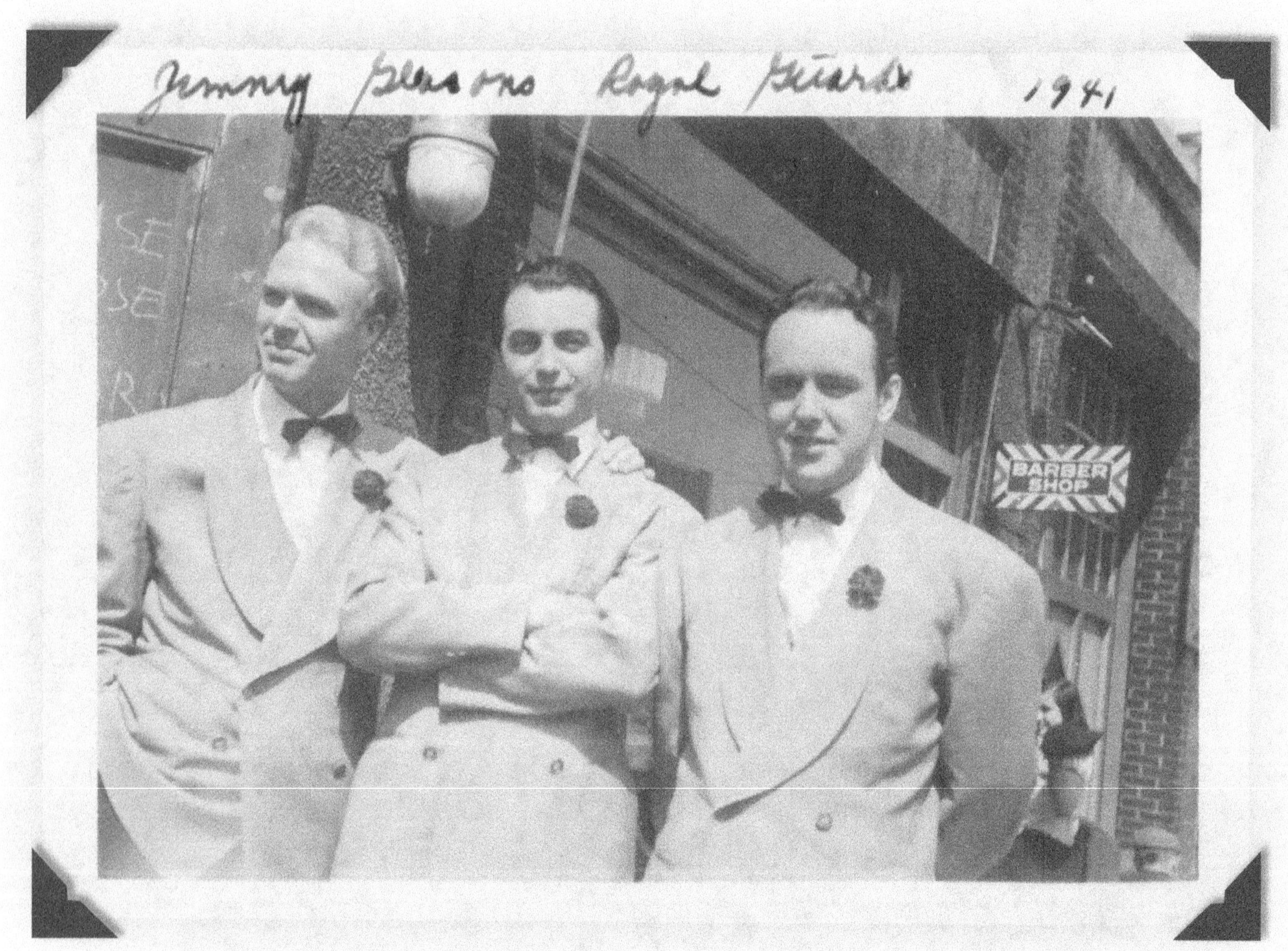

Jimmy Gleason's Royal Guards   1941
BARBER SHOP

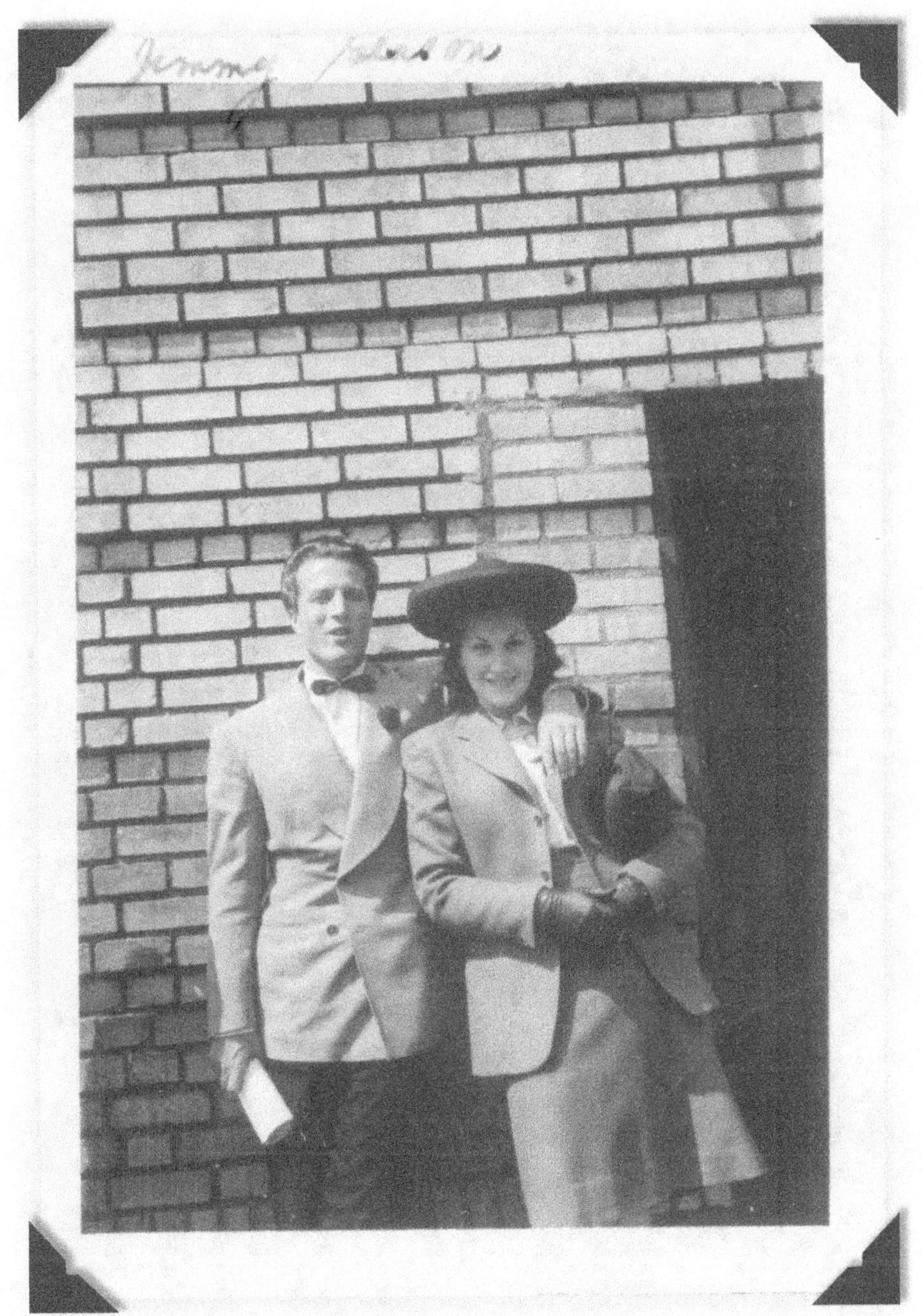

Jimmy Johnson

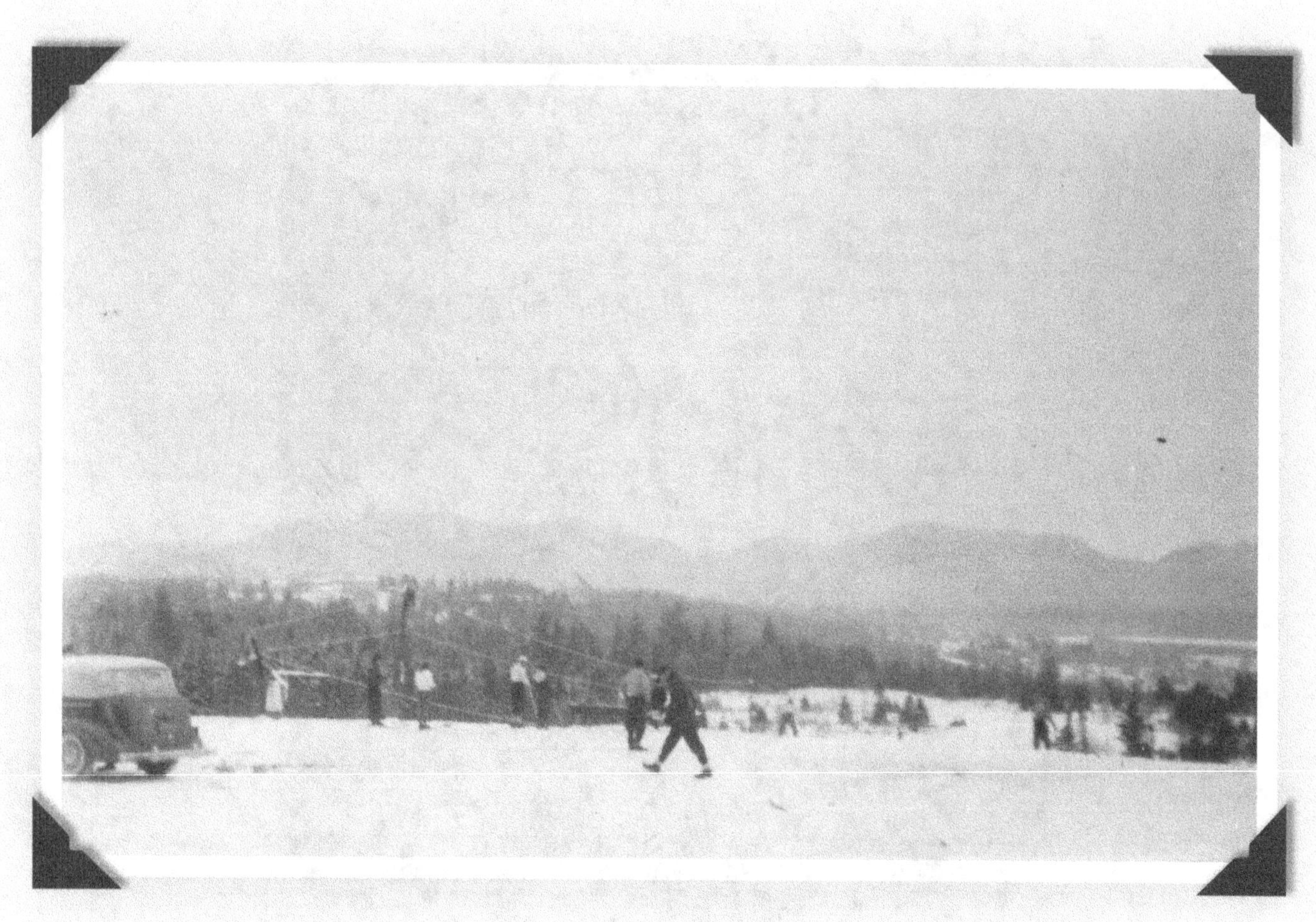

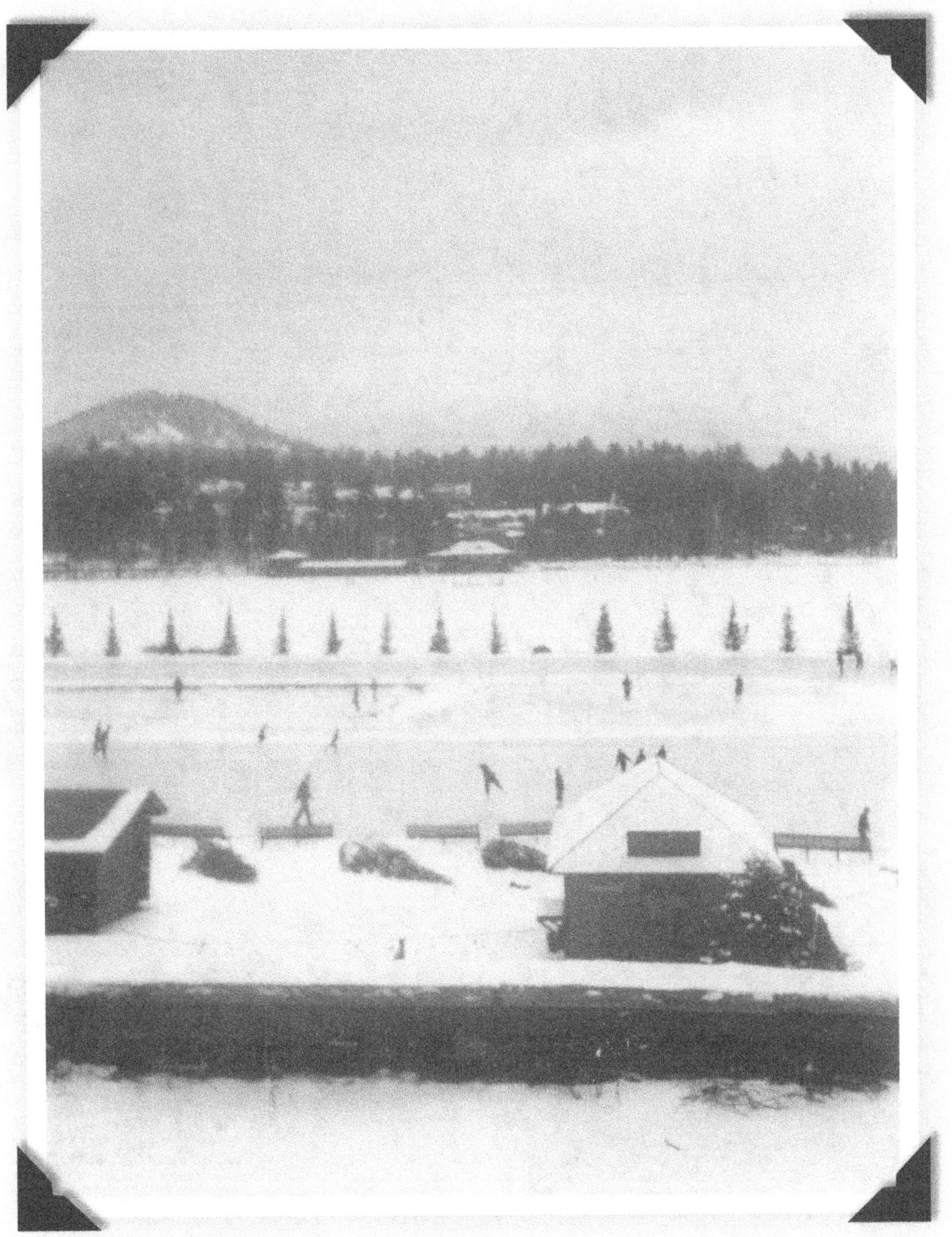

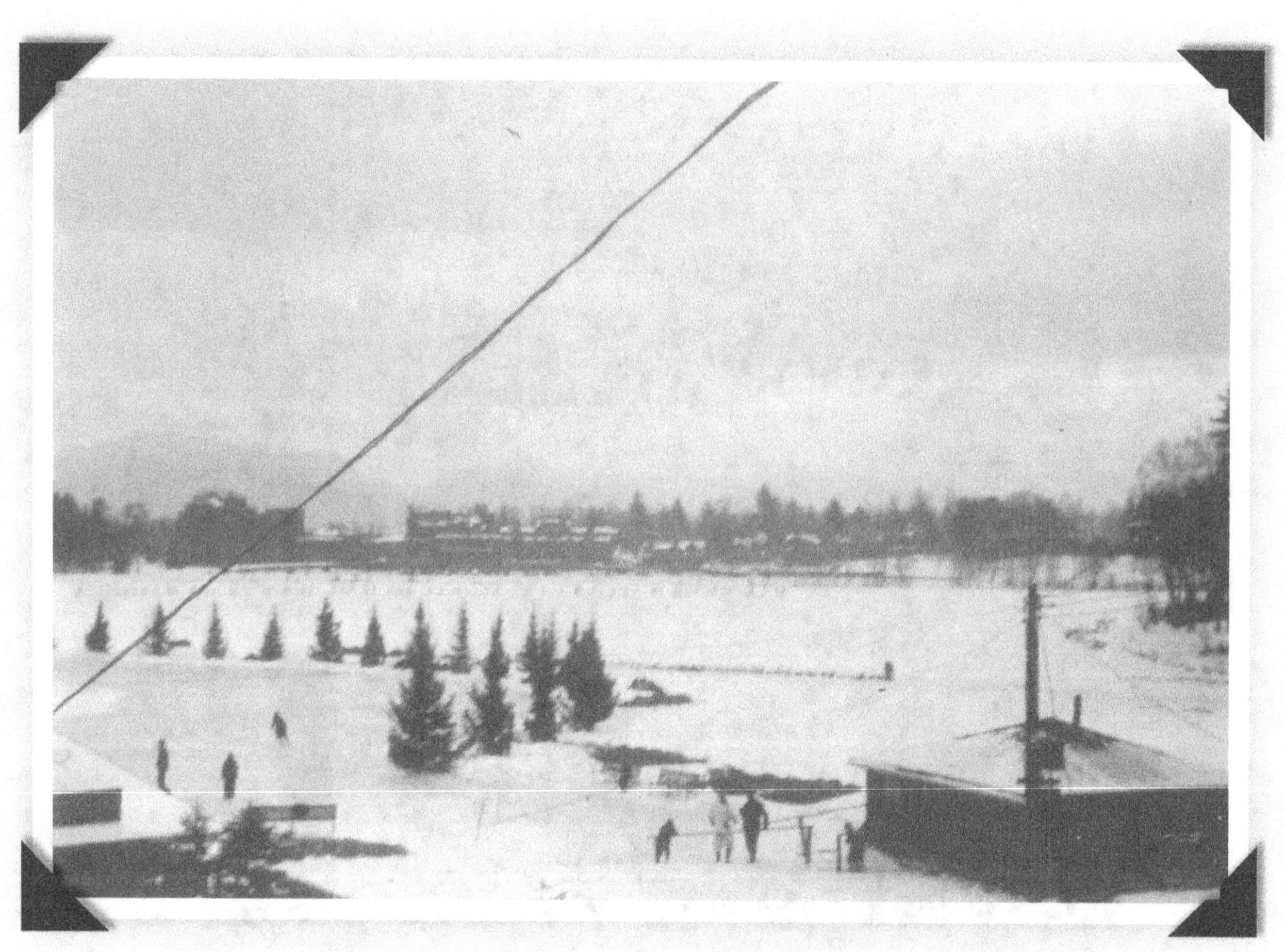

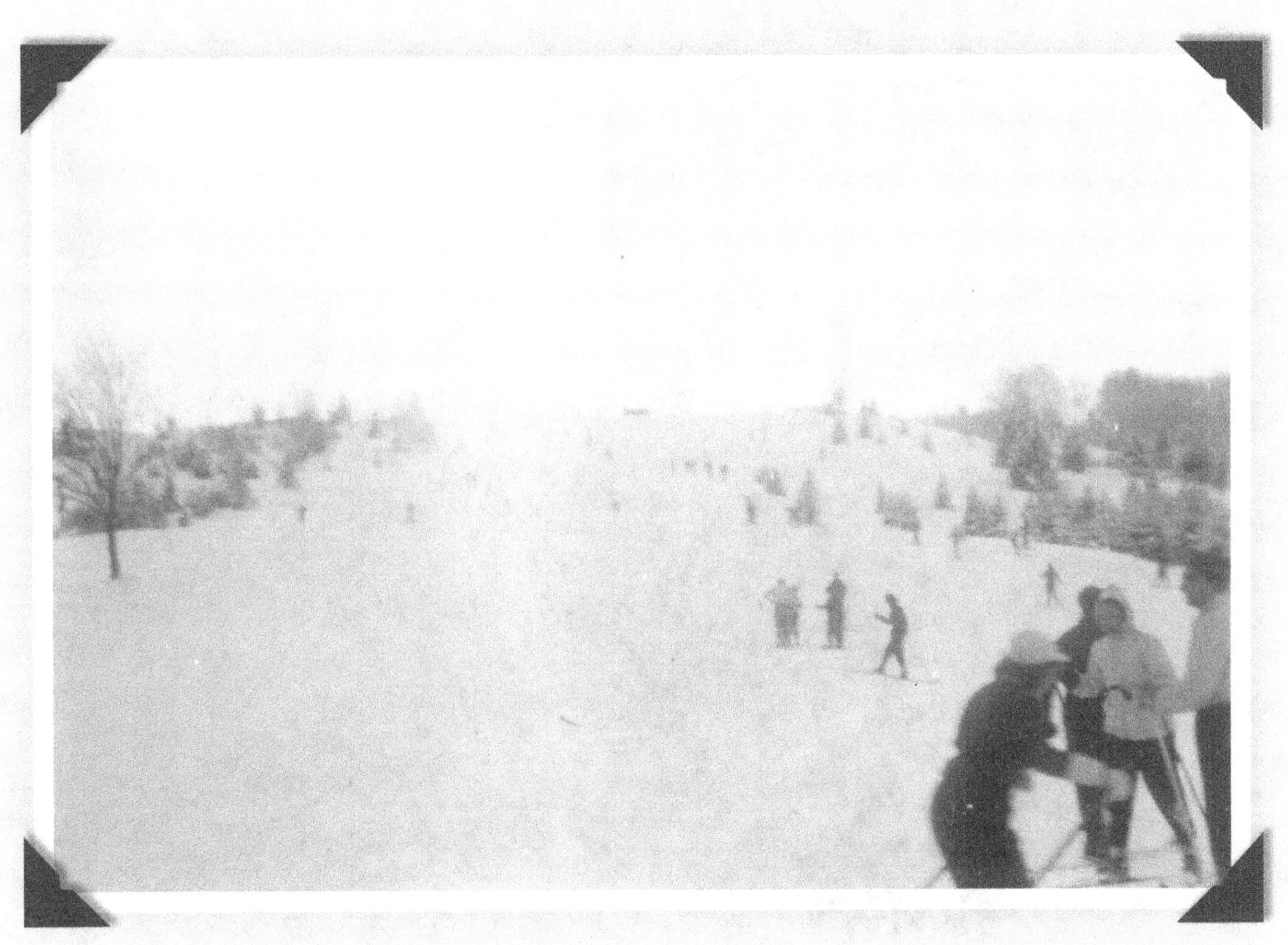

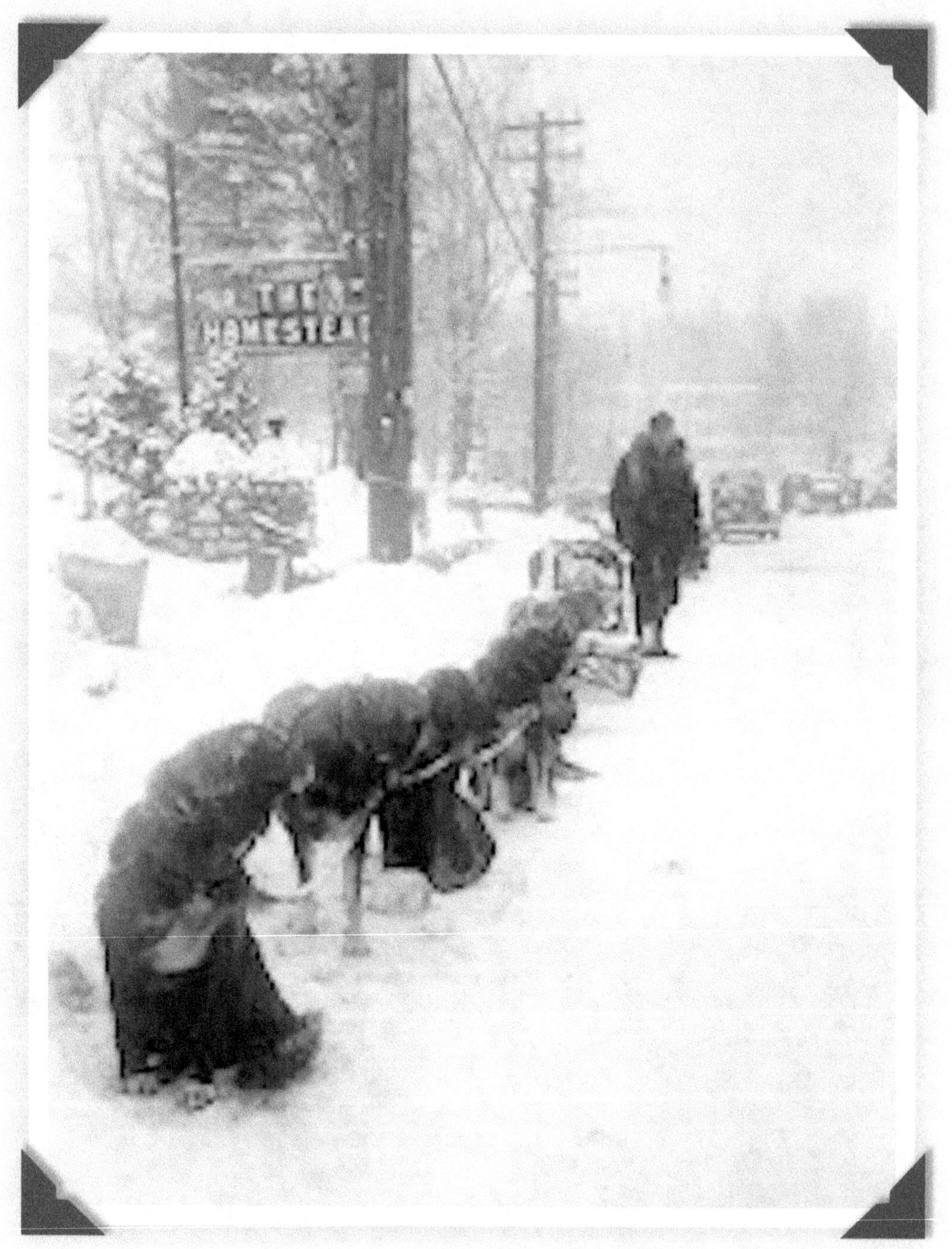
THE
HOMESTEAD

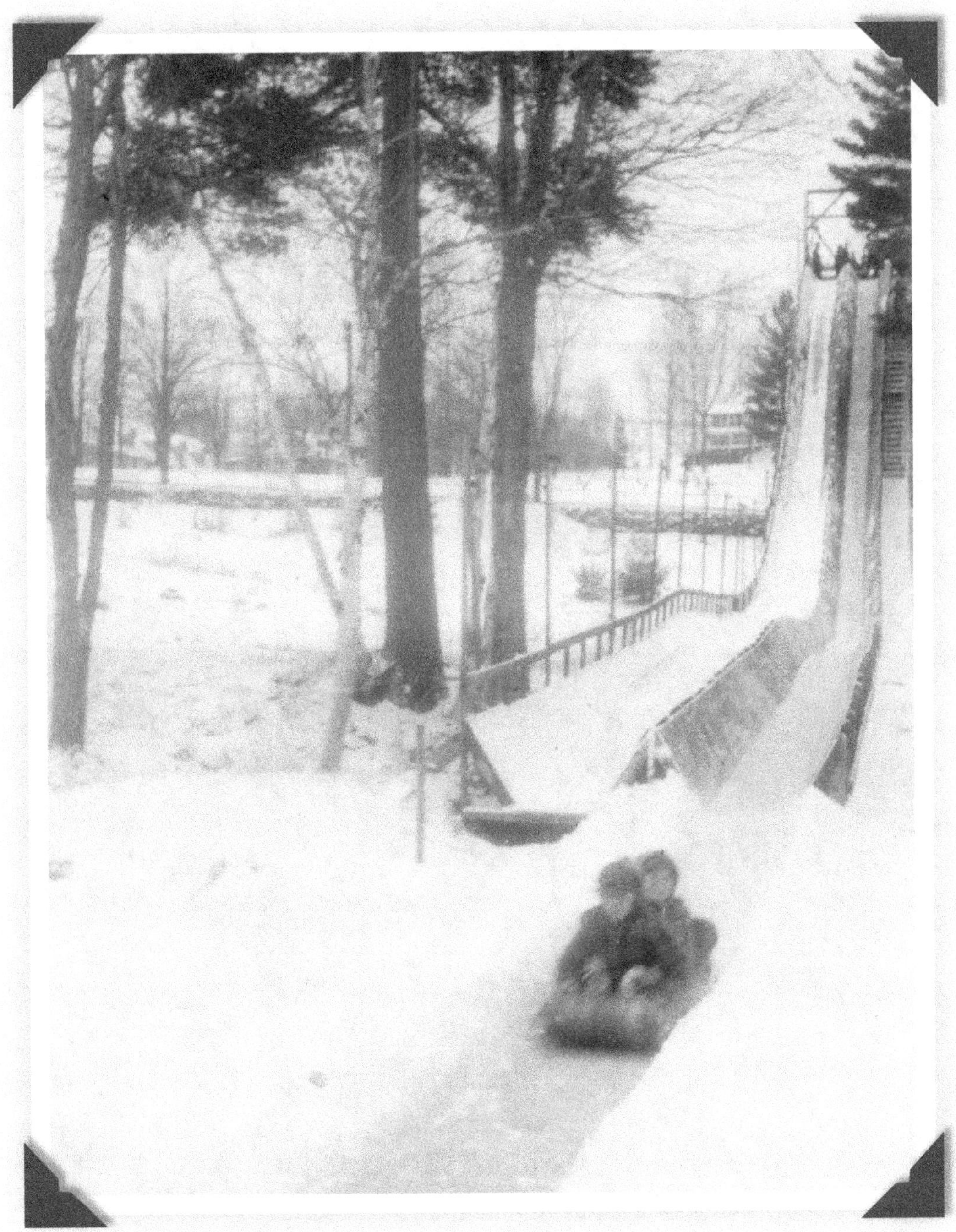

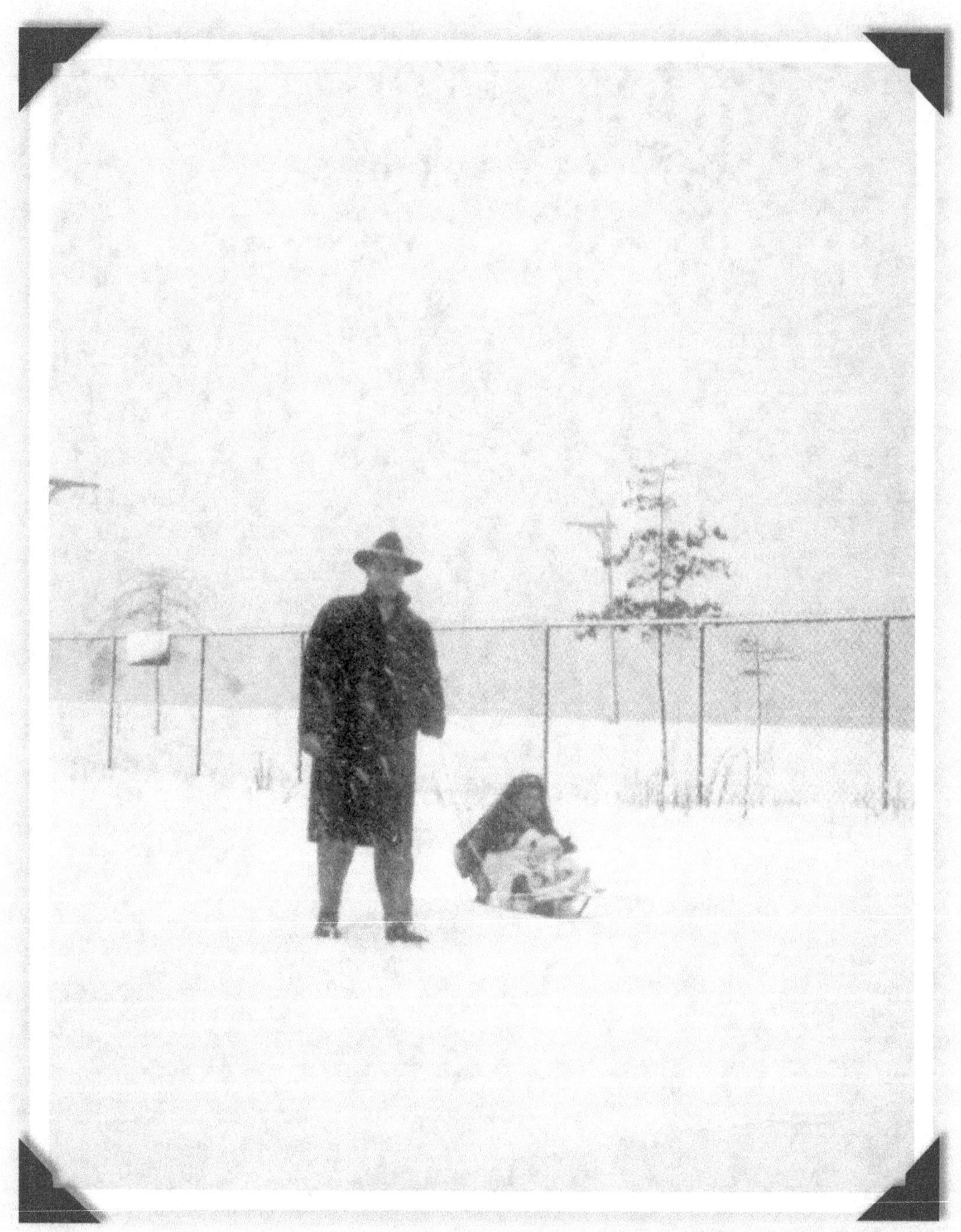

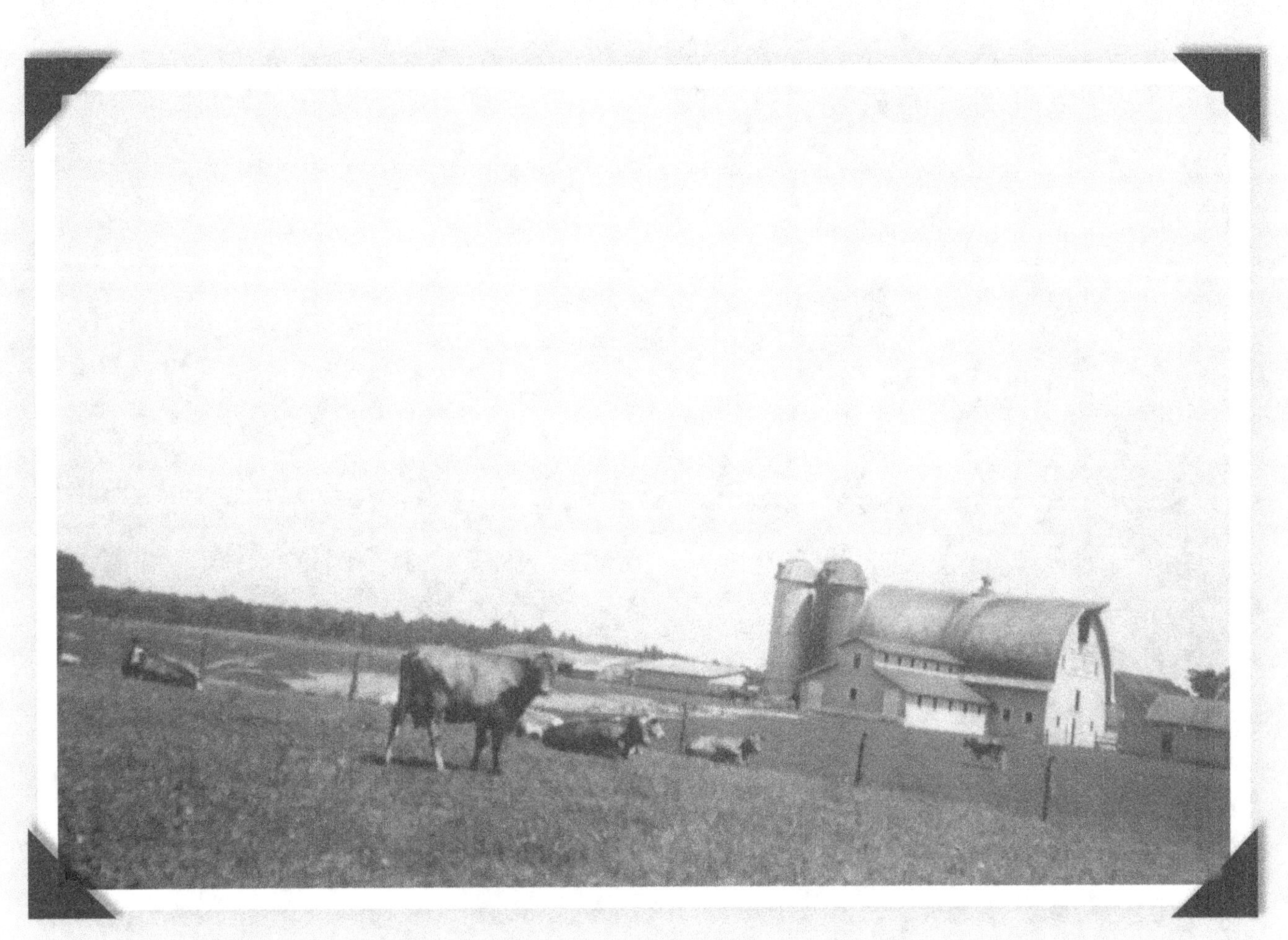

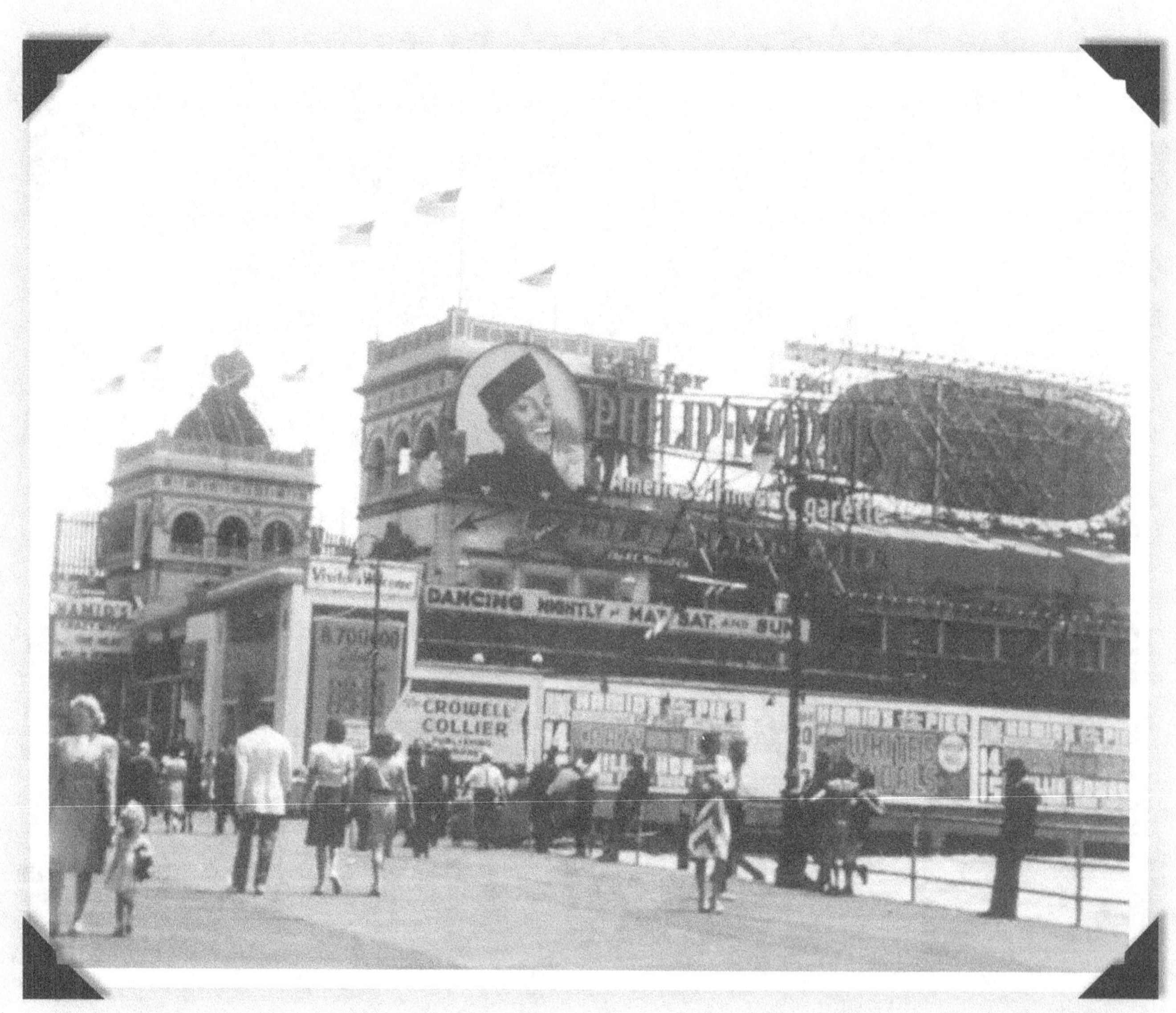

PHILIP MORRIS
garette
DANCING NIGHTLY
CROWELL
COLLIER

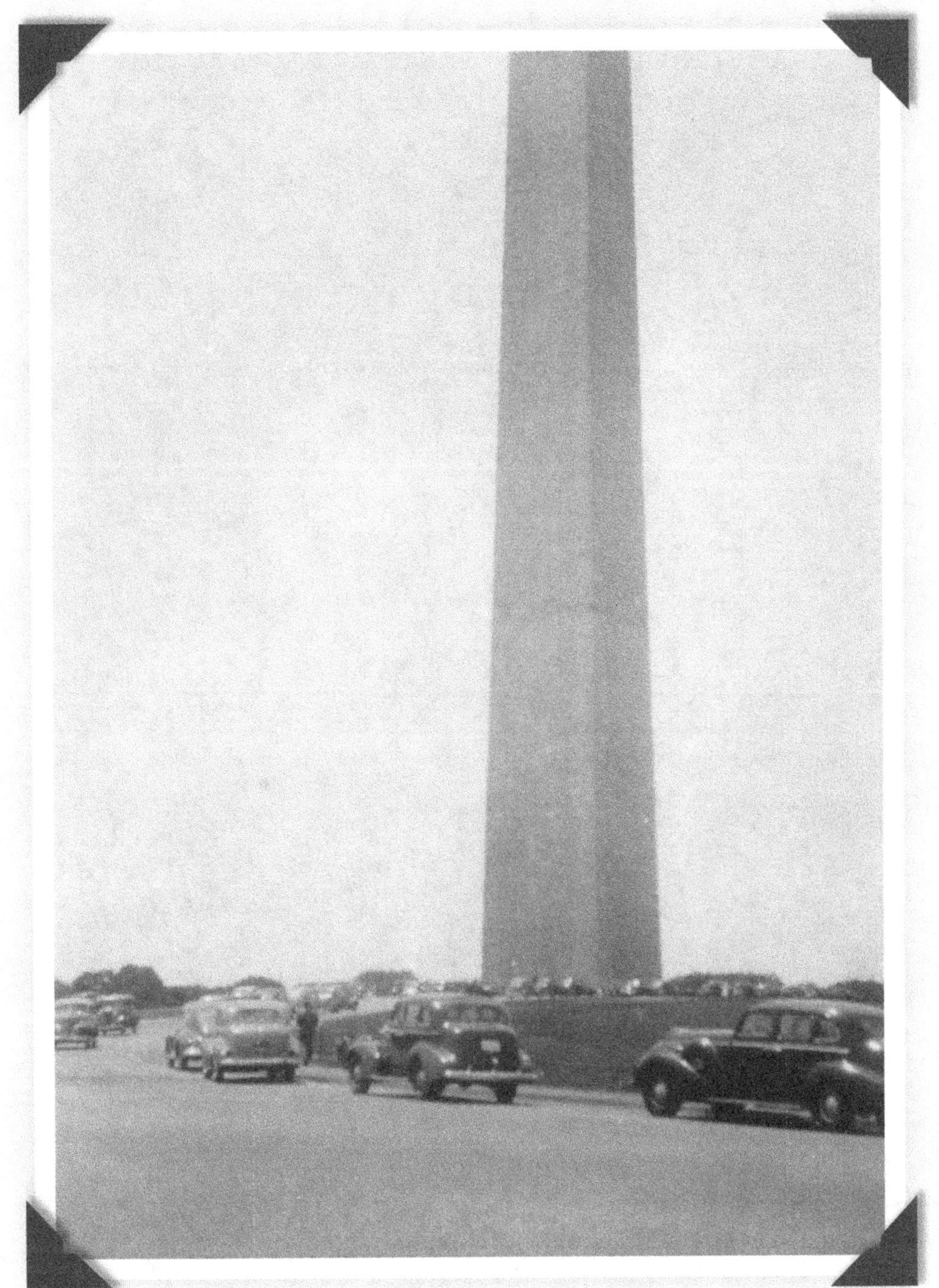

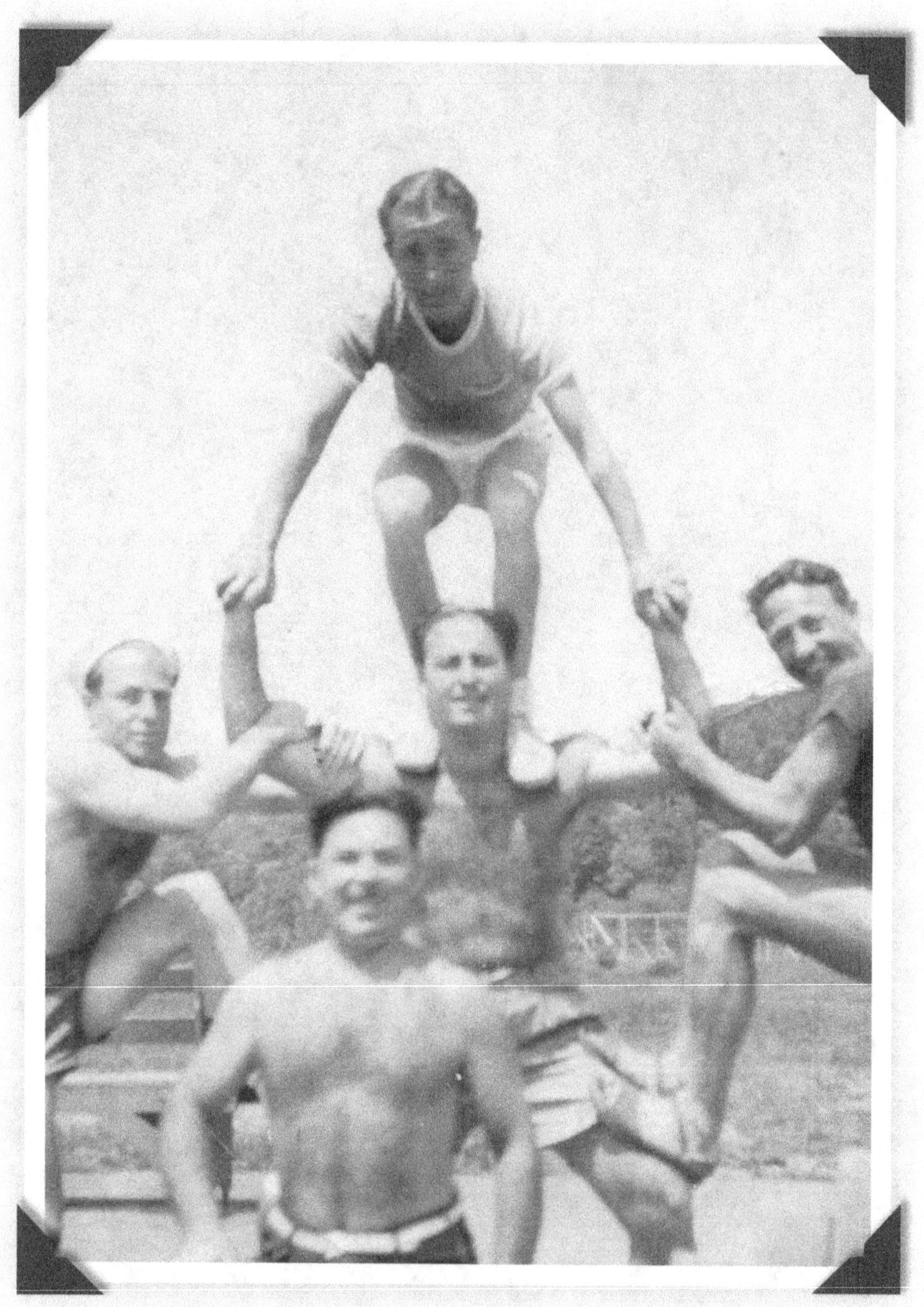

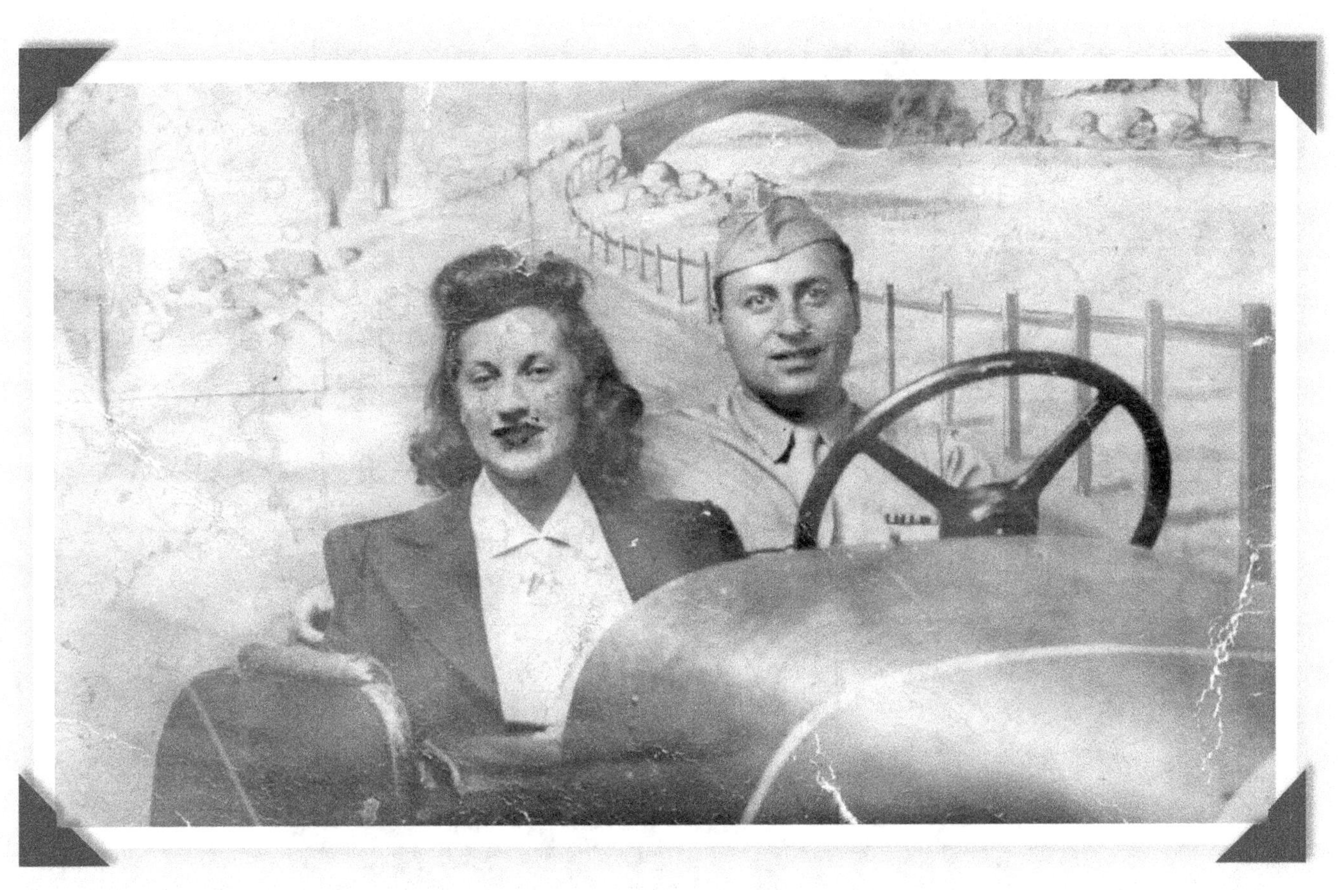

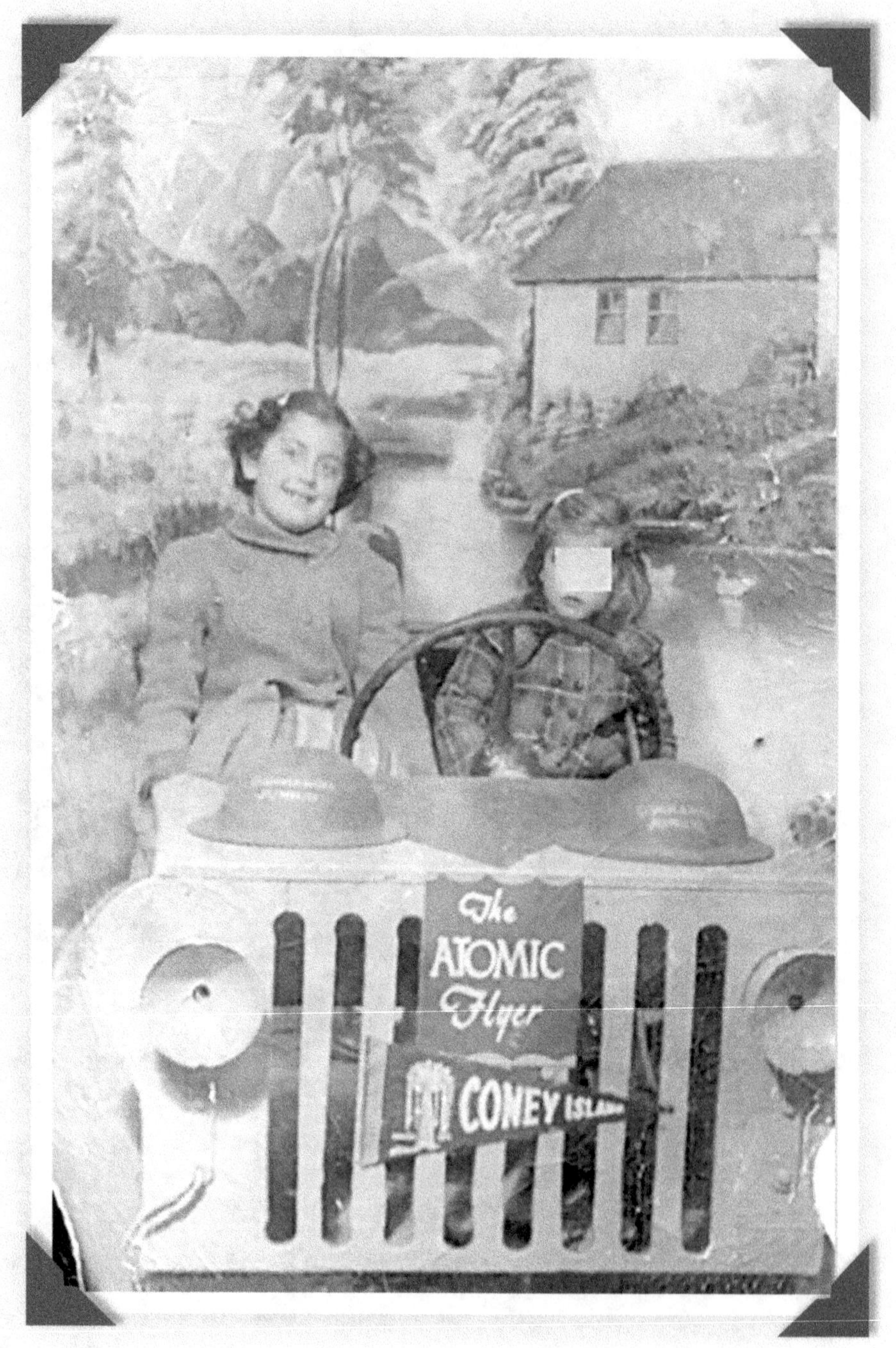

The
ATOMIC
Flyer
CONEY ISLAND

THE MIDDLE GROUND

With one breath in these photos, I can revisit times in
old photo booths, beach clubs, summer camps,
family trips, and my dated high hair…
which delineated my teen scenes.

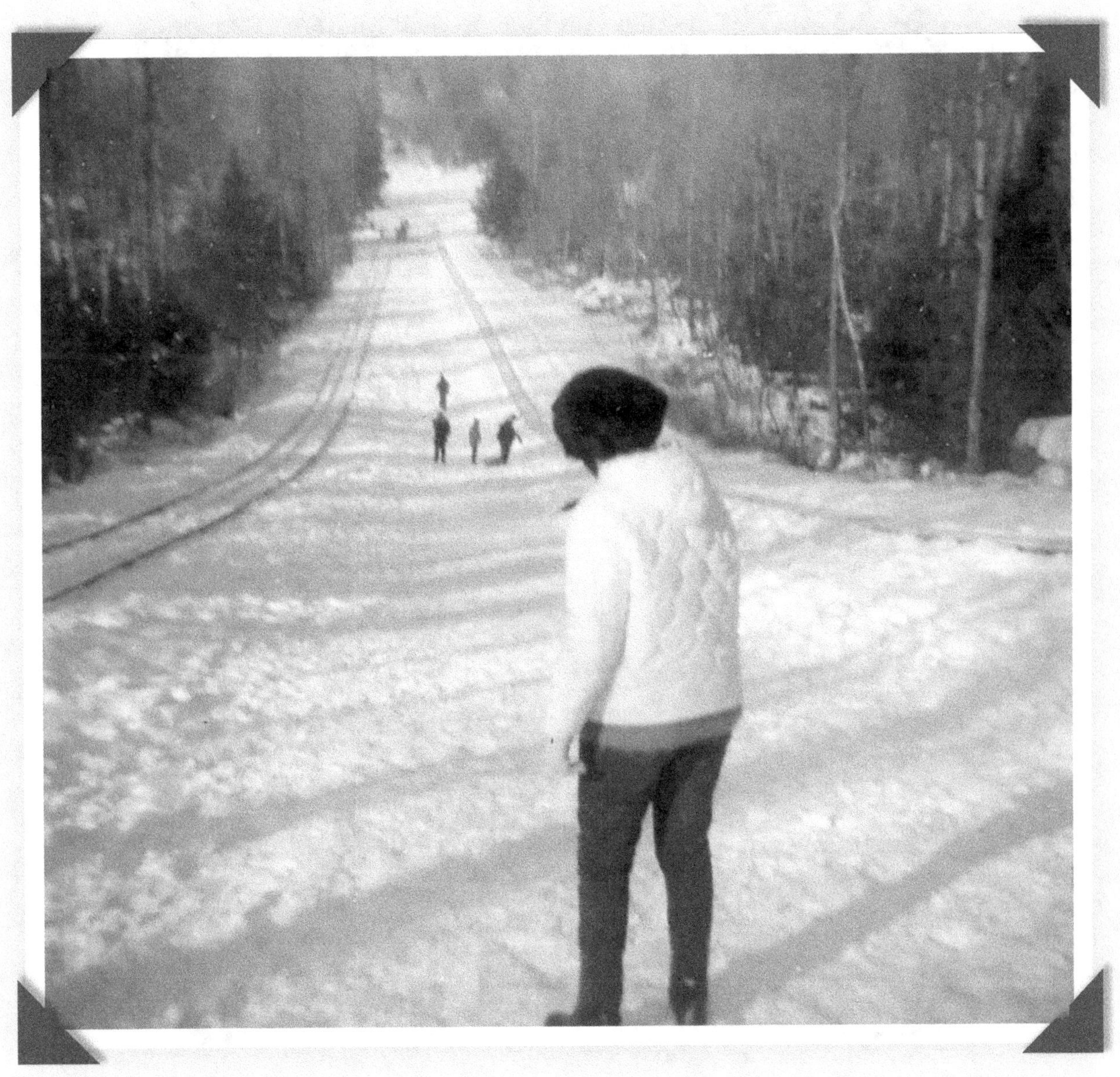

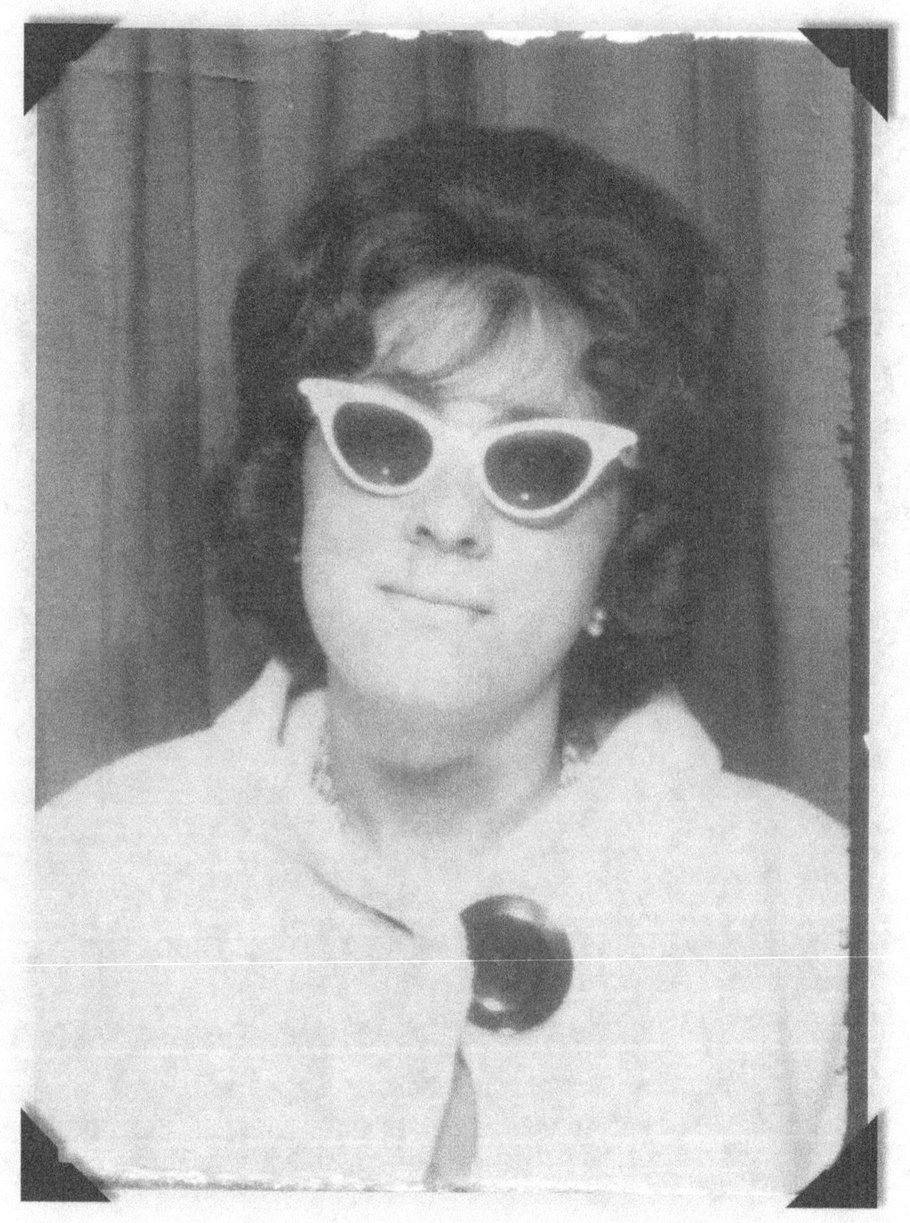

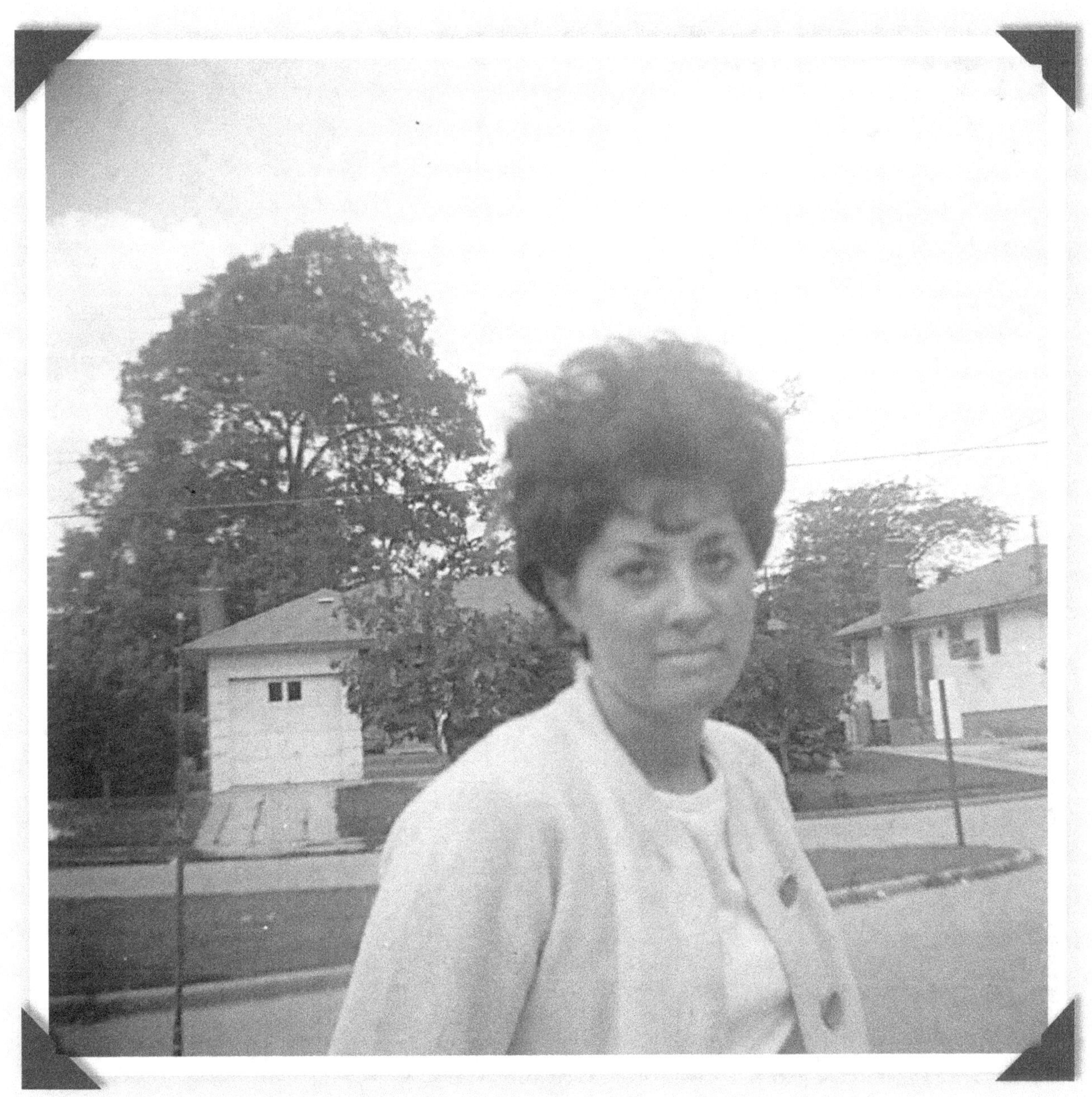

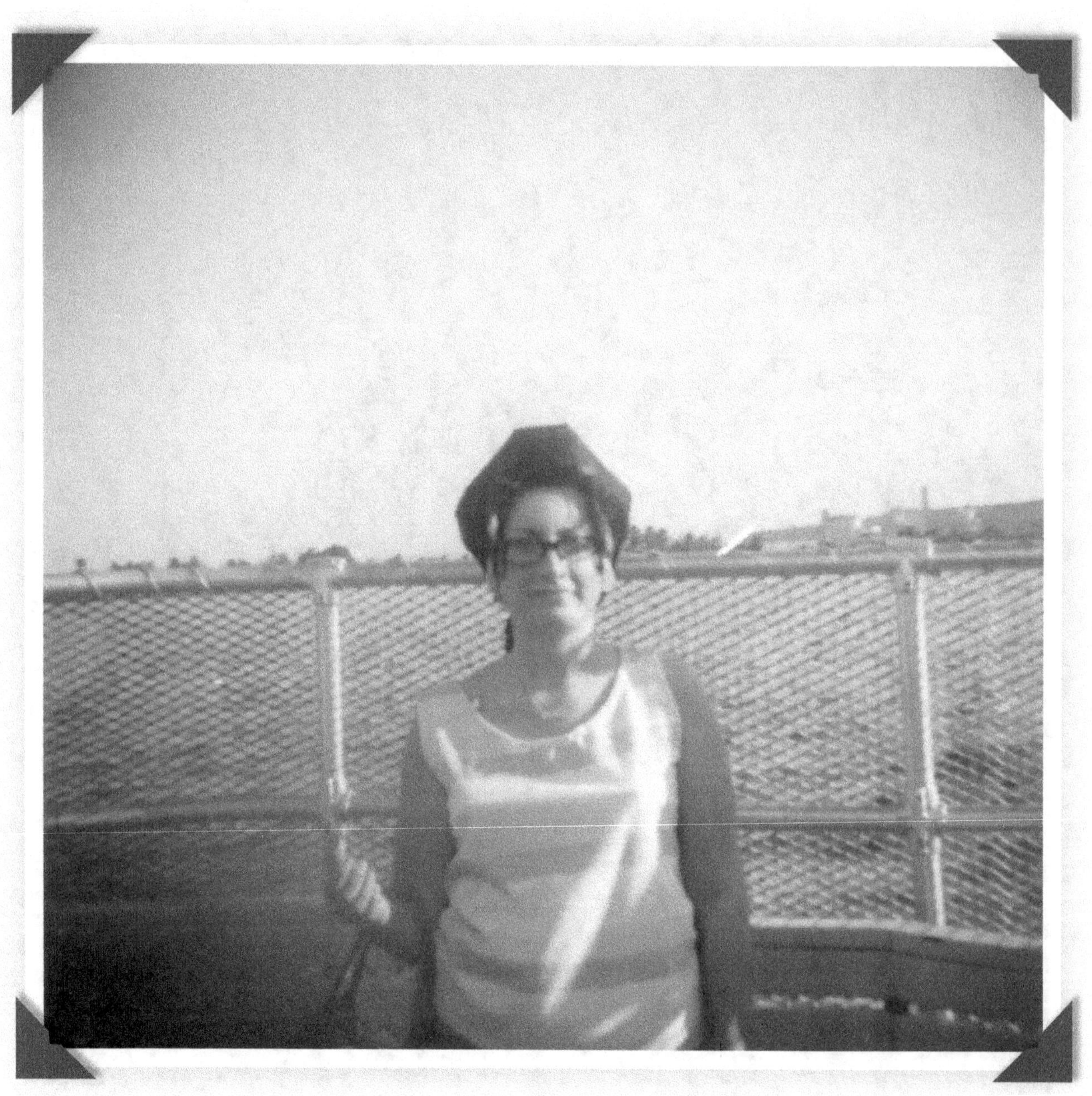

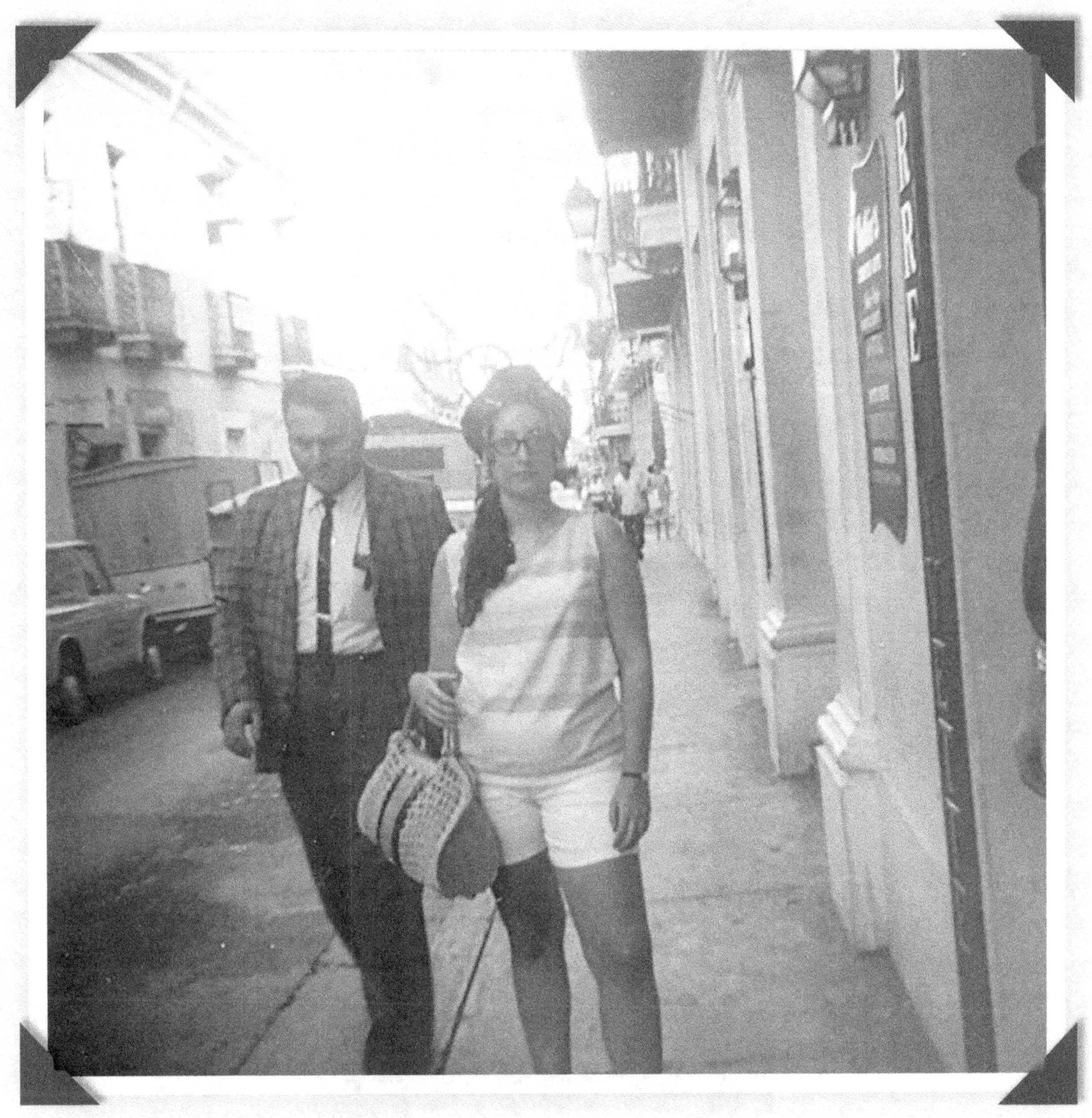

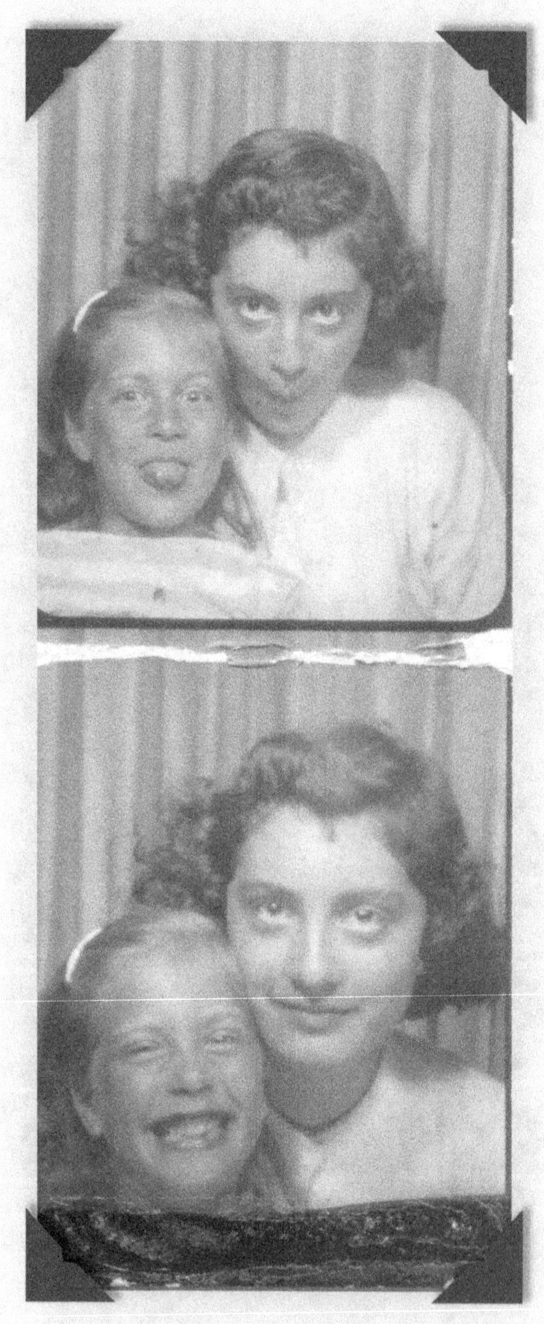

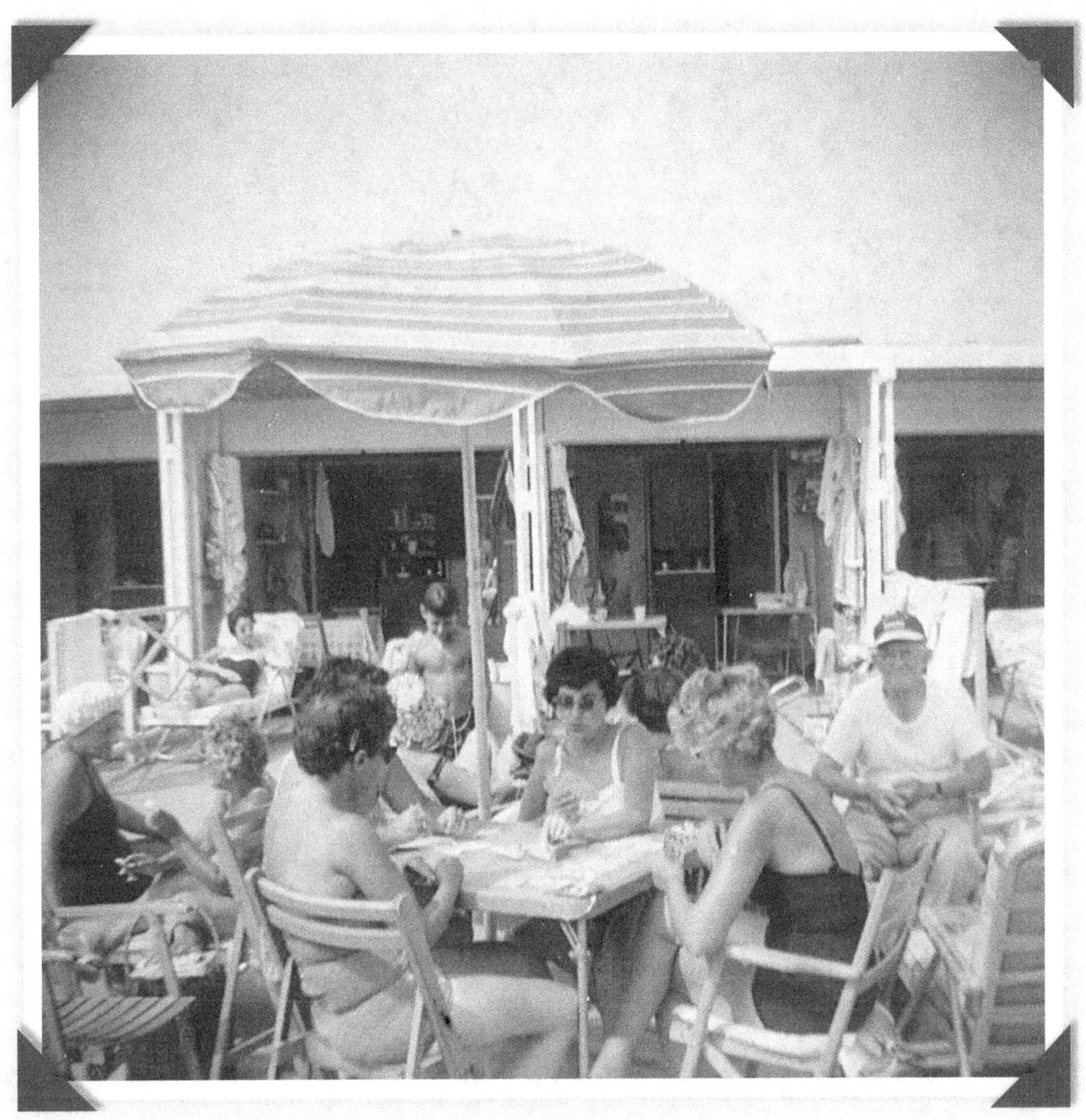

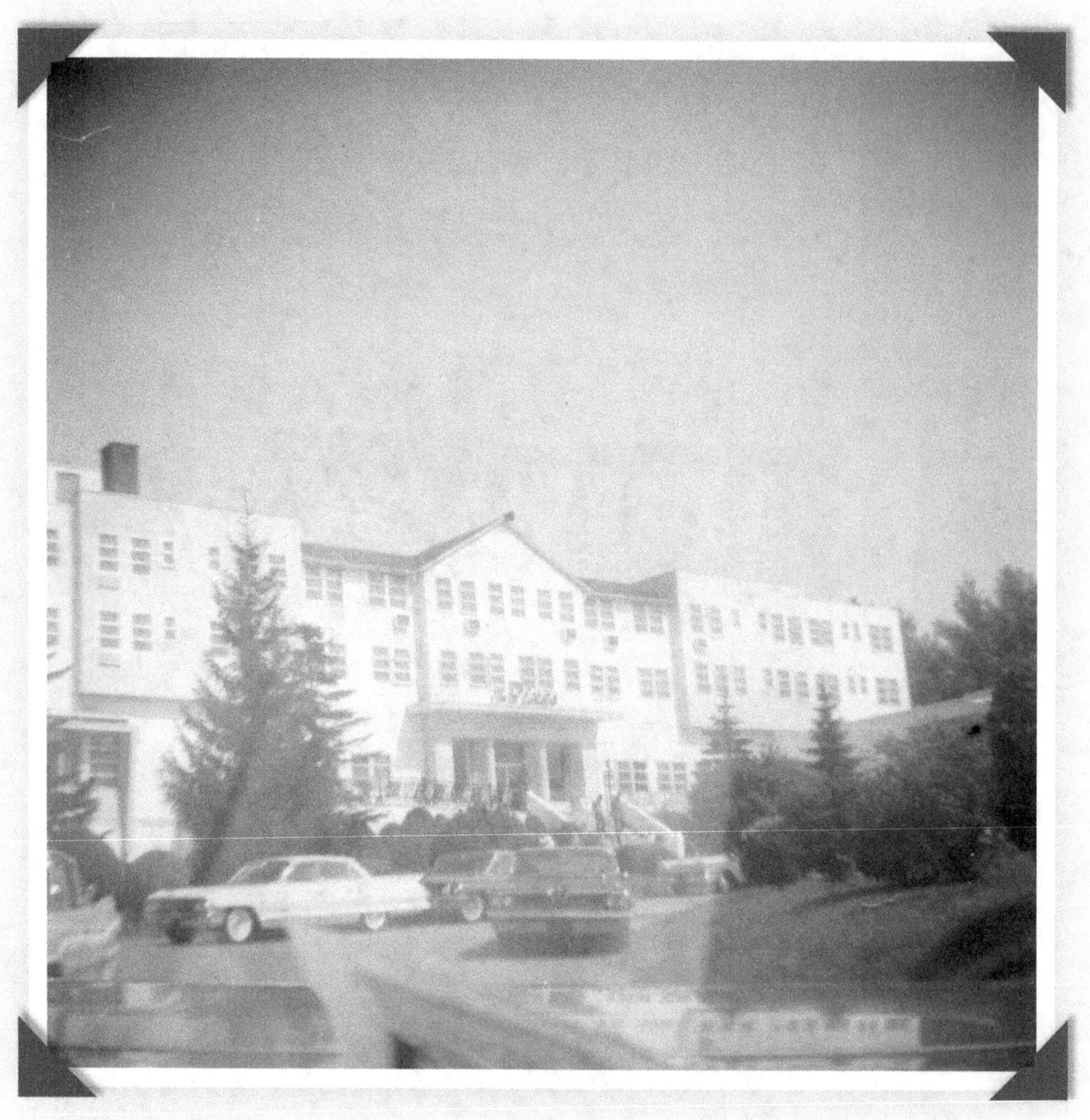

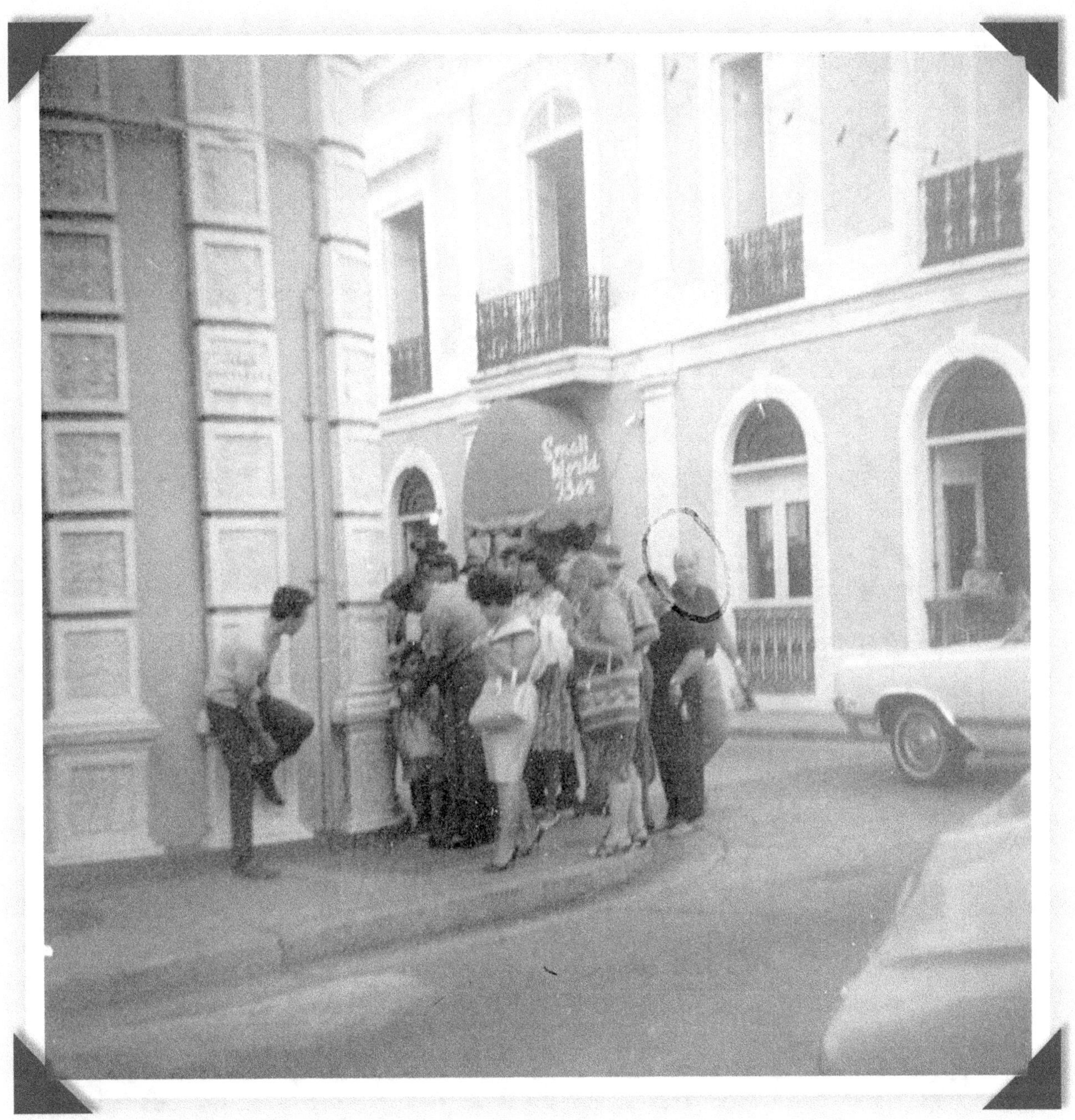

Small
World
Bar

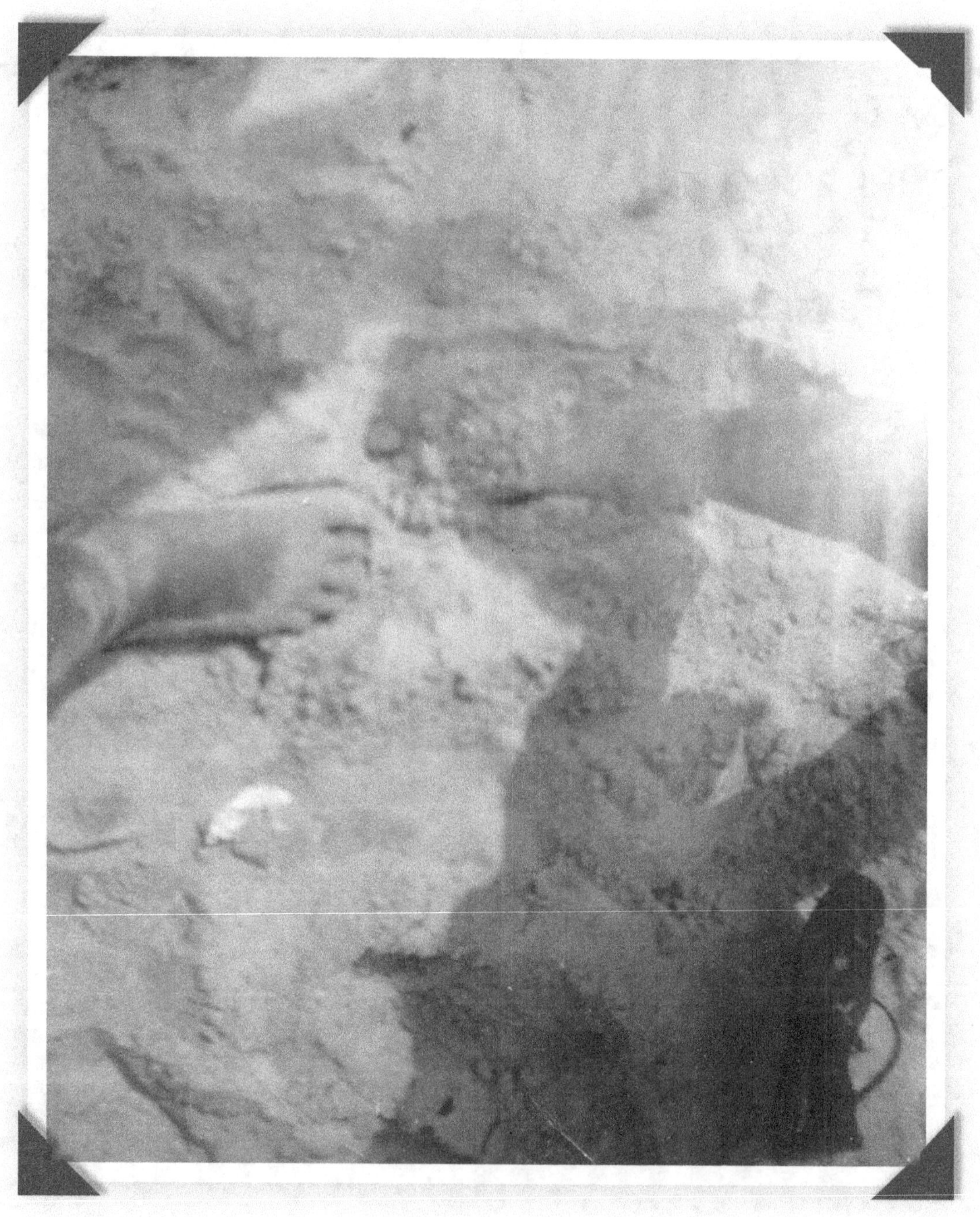

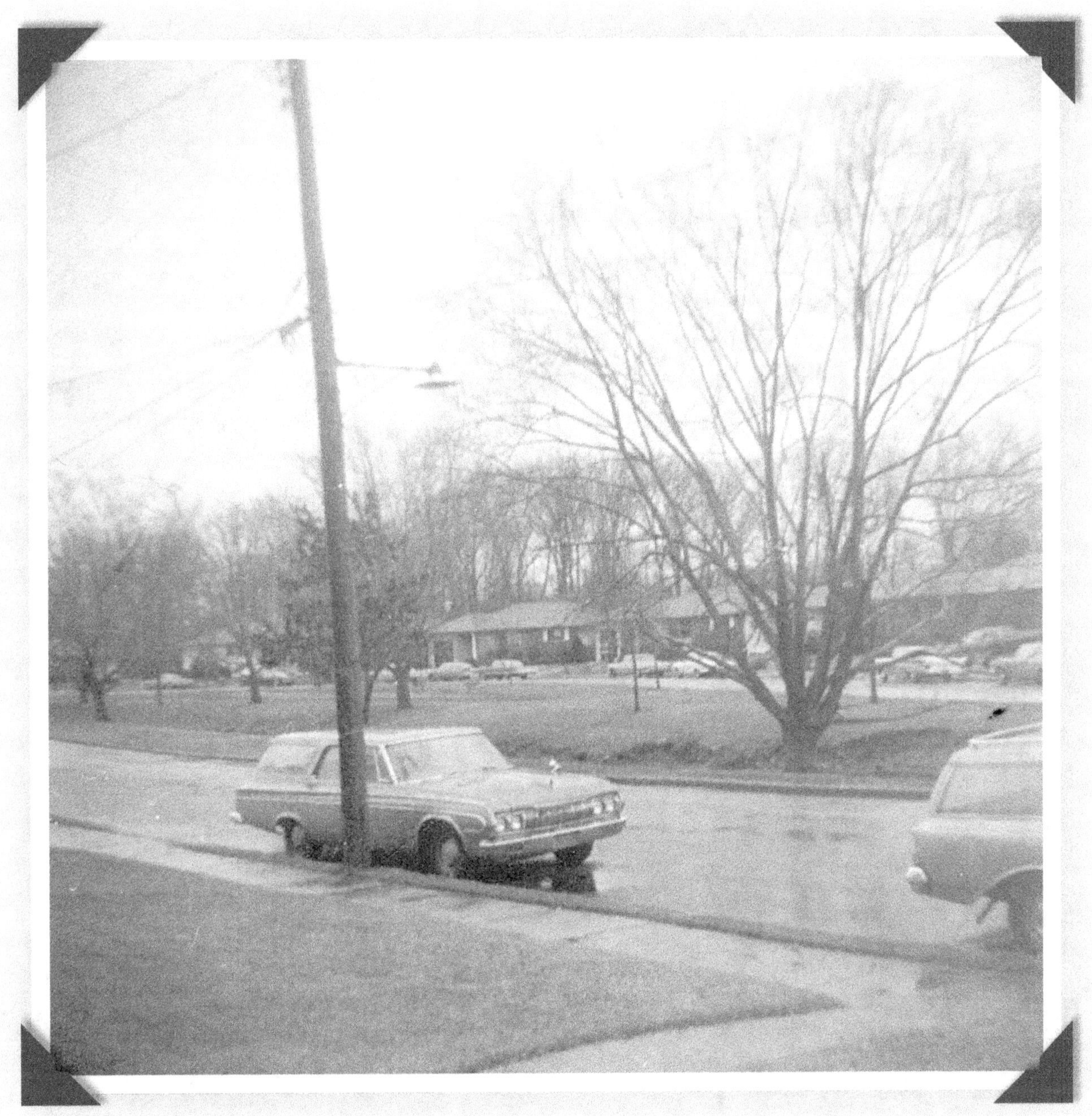

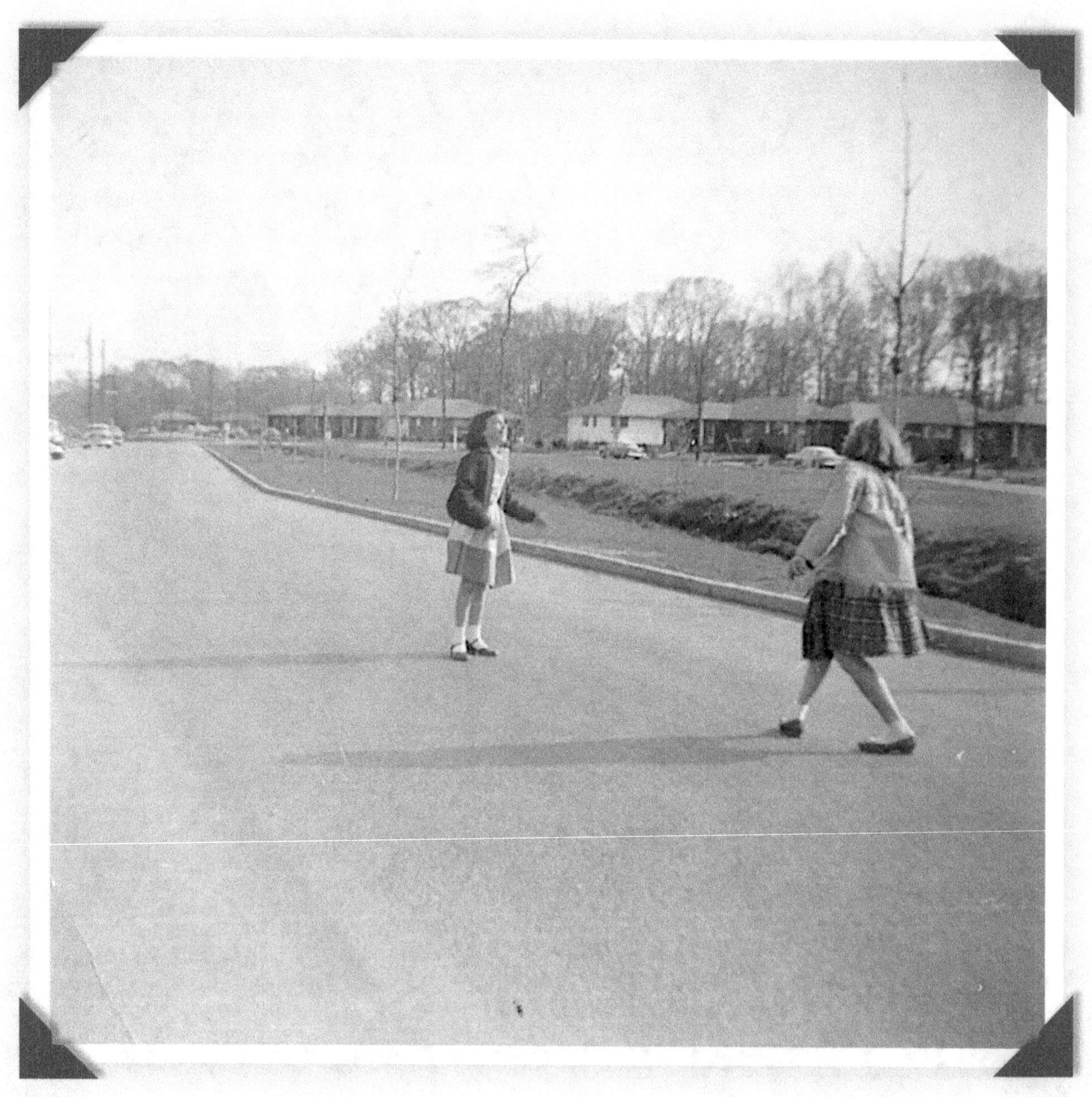

78 ~ from THE ATTIC

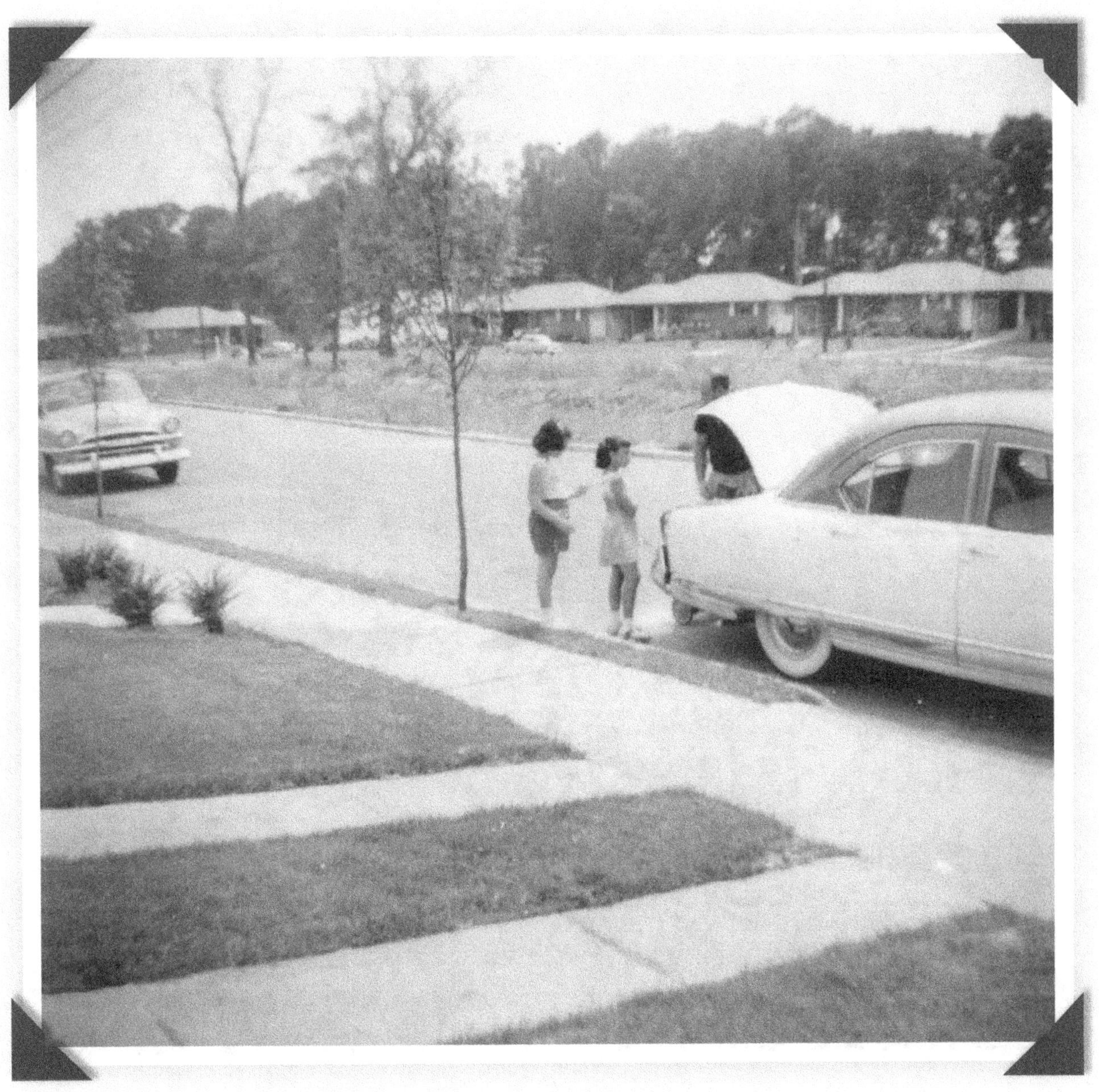

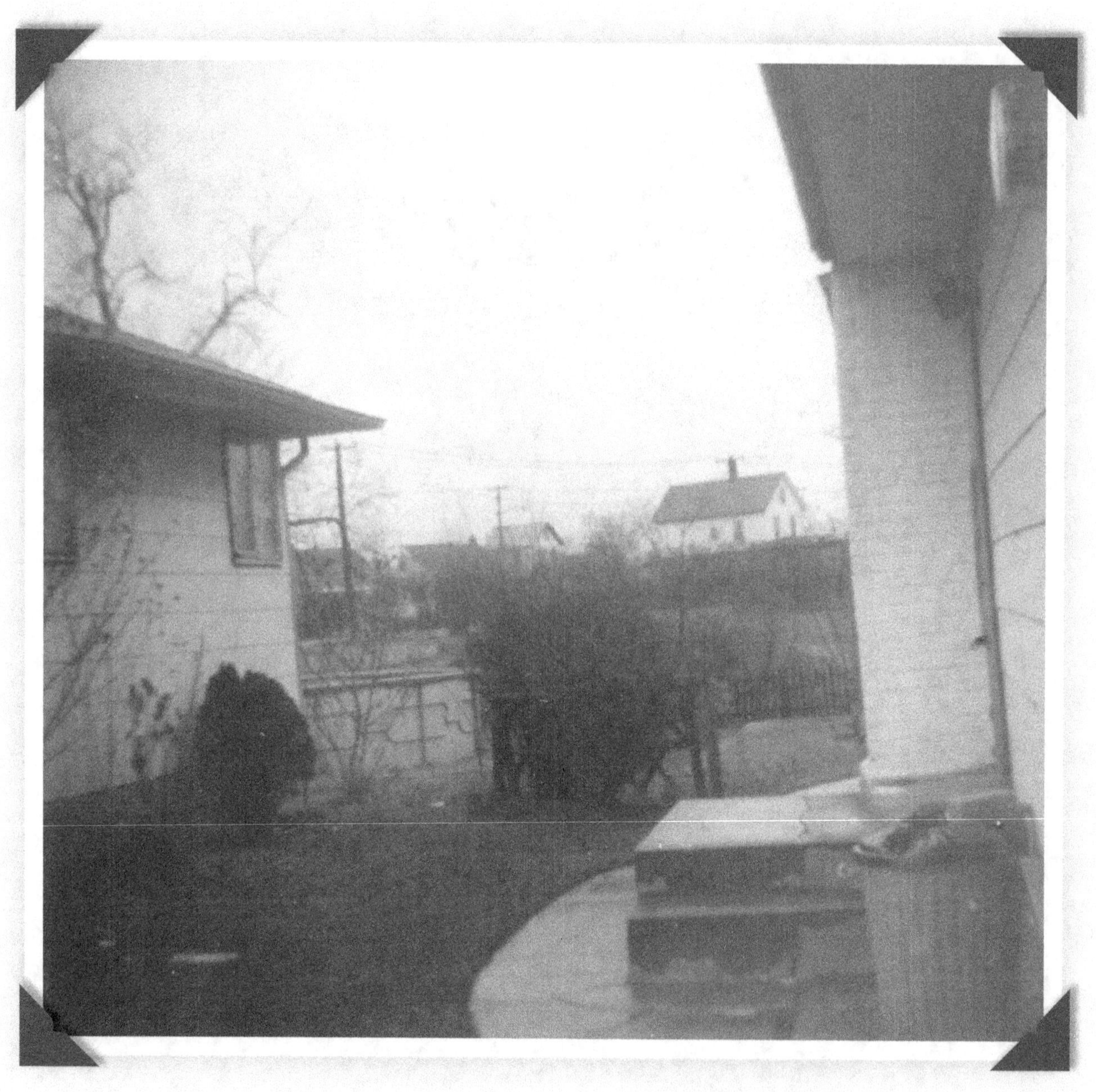

80 ~ from THE ATTIC

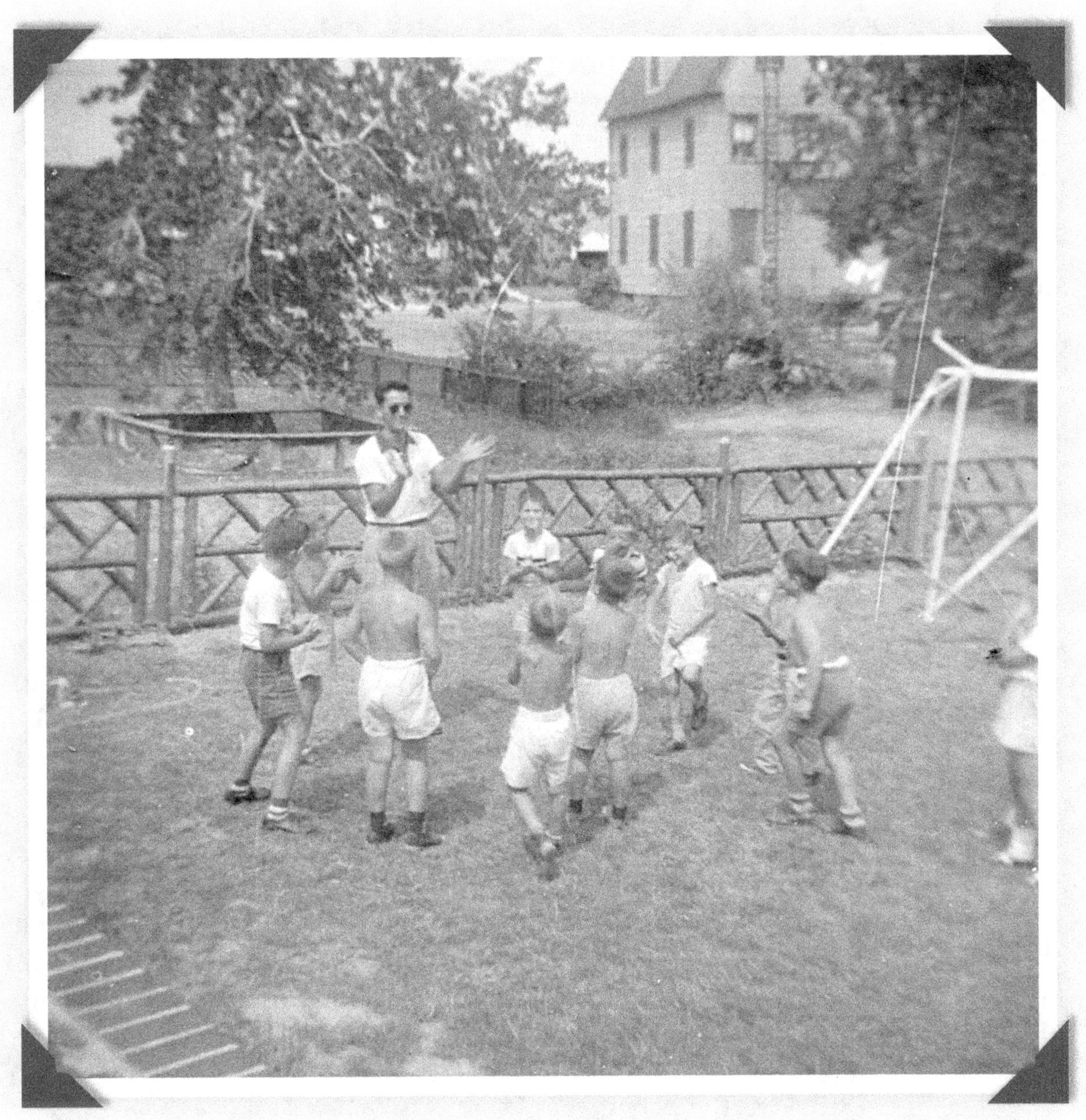

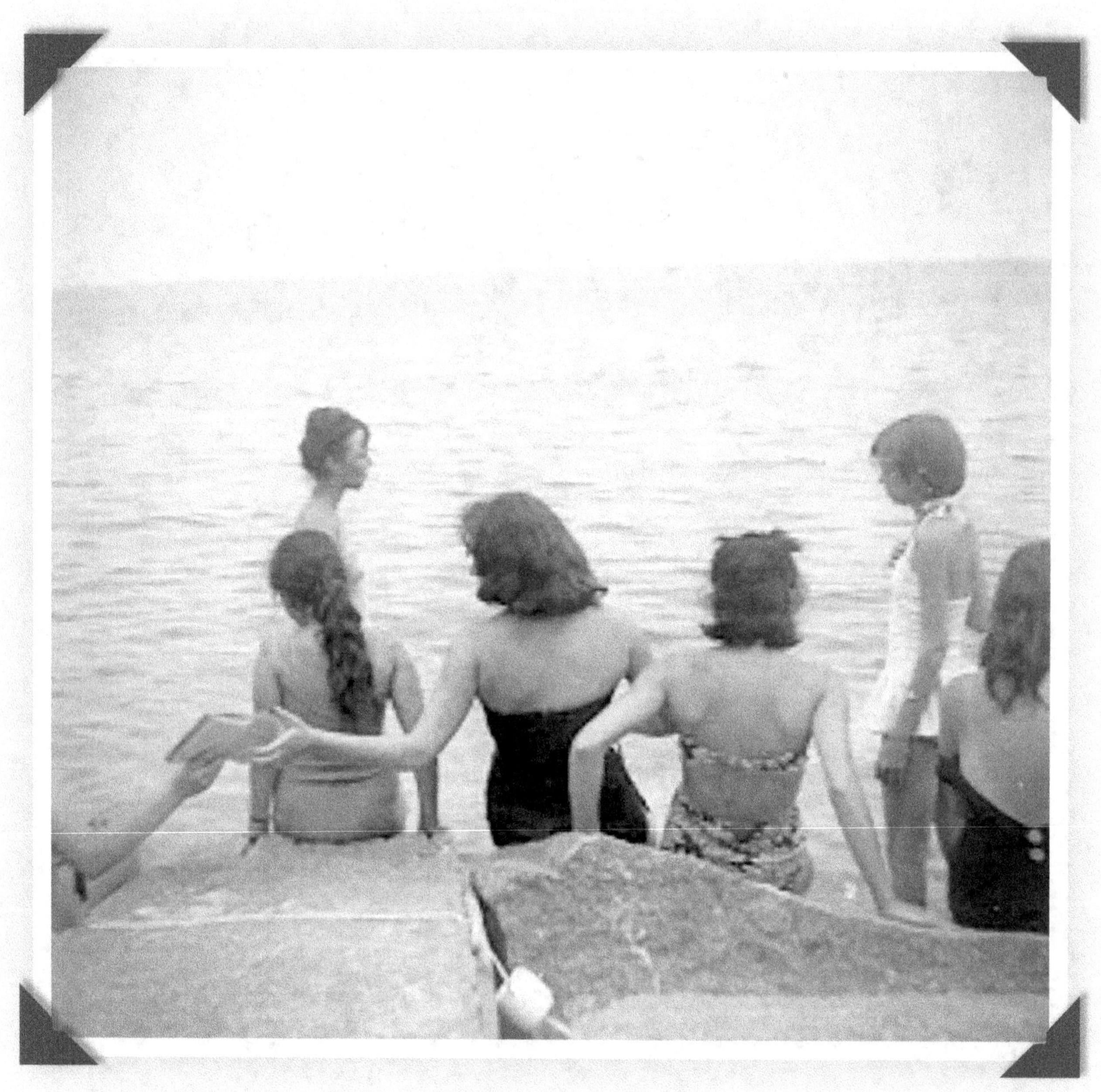

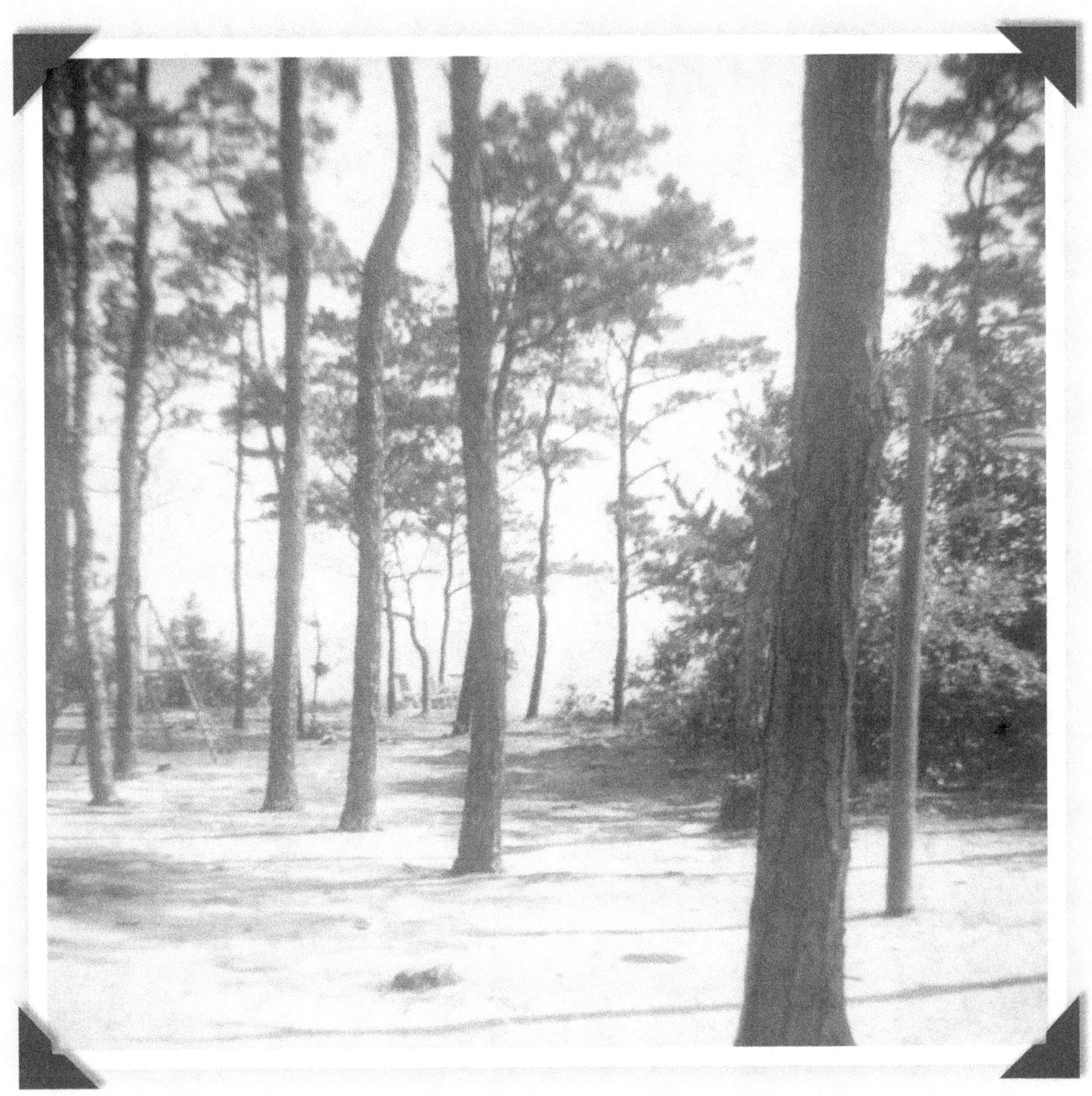

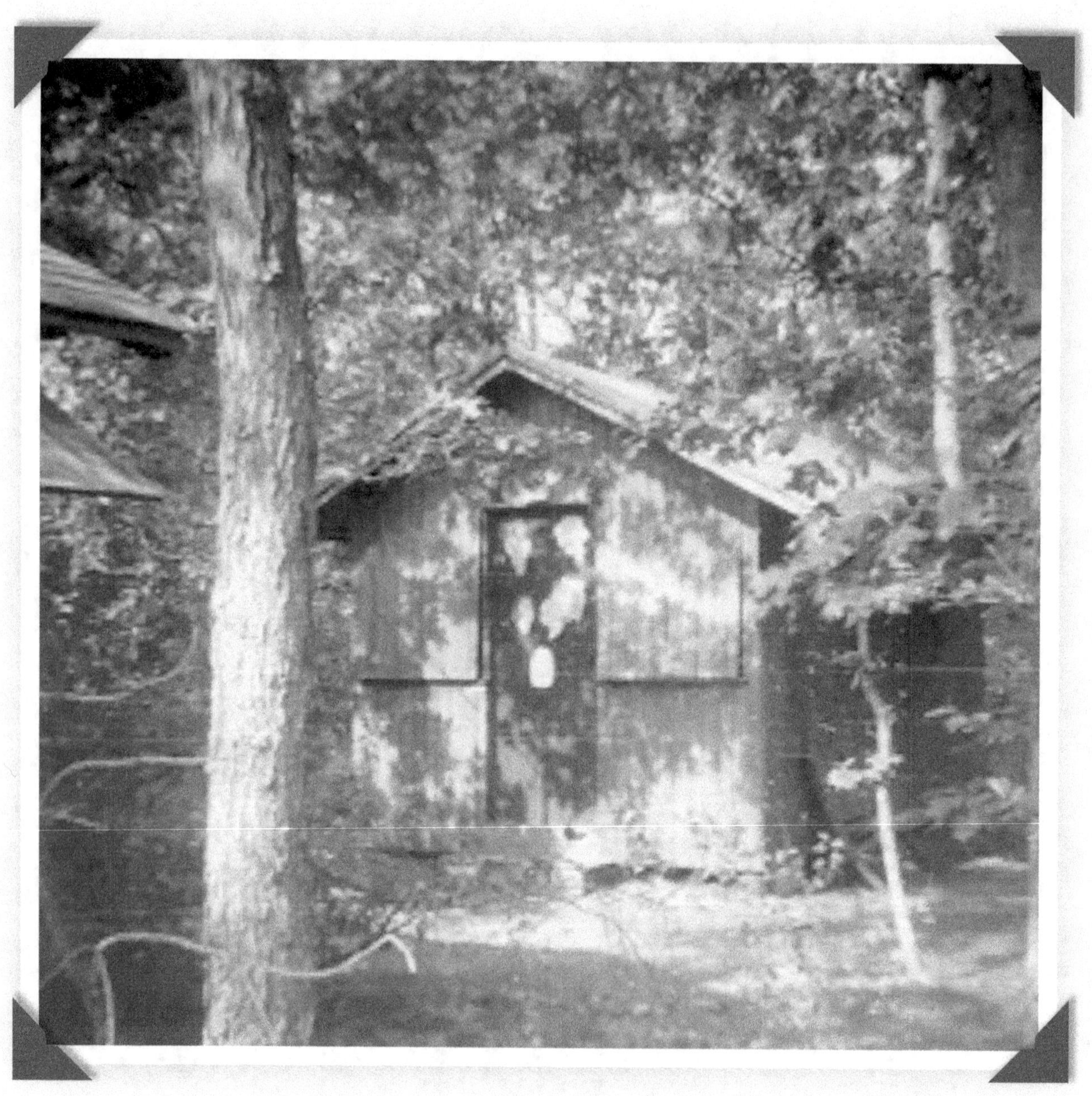

THE WWII ARMY YEARS

My father was stationed in the Aleutian Islands of Alaska during WWII and he left me a treasure trove of memorabilia which is represented in this collection.

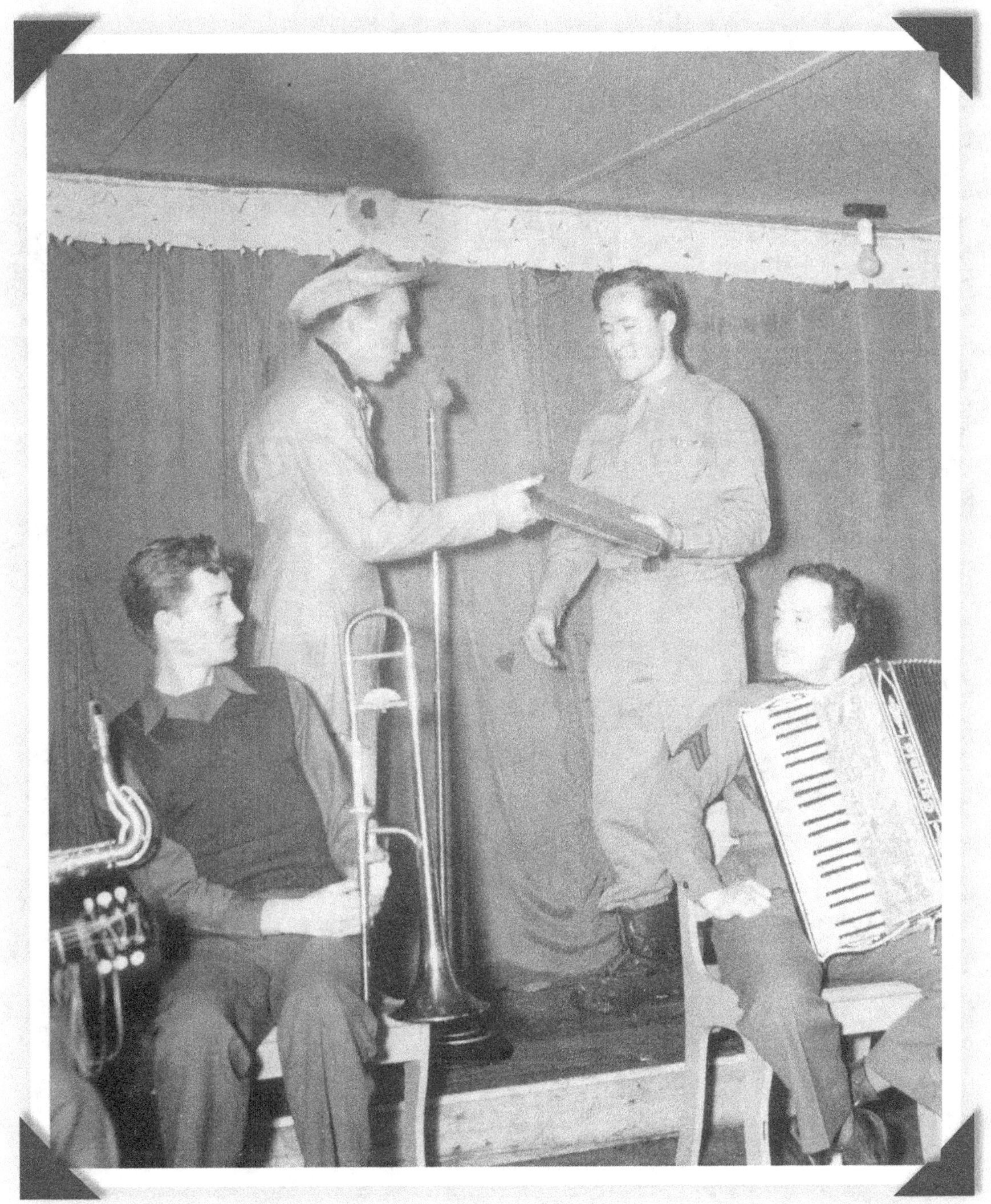

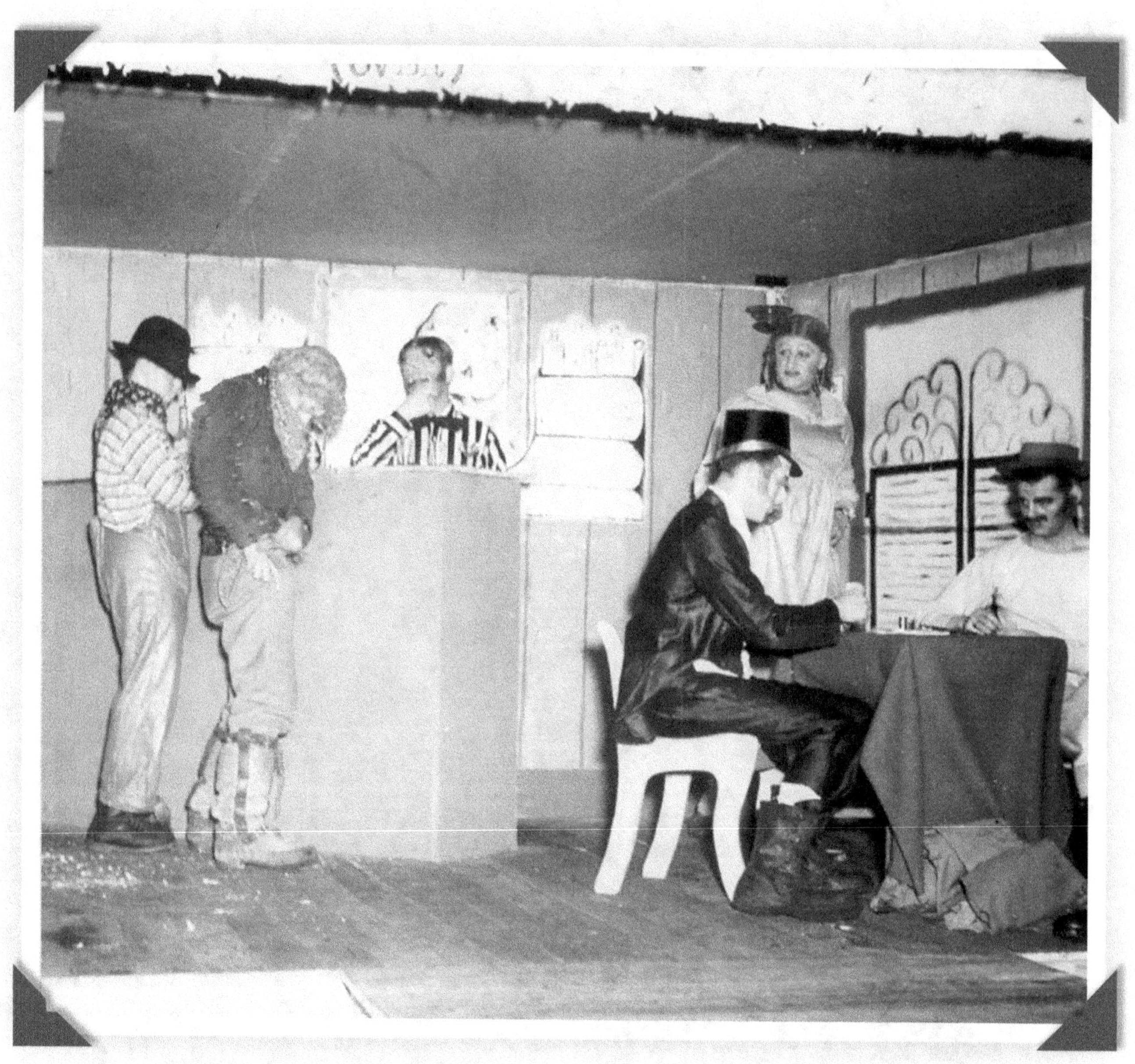

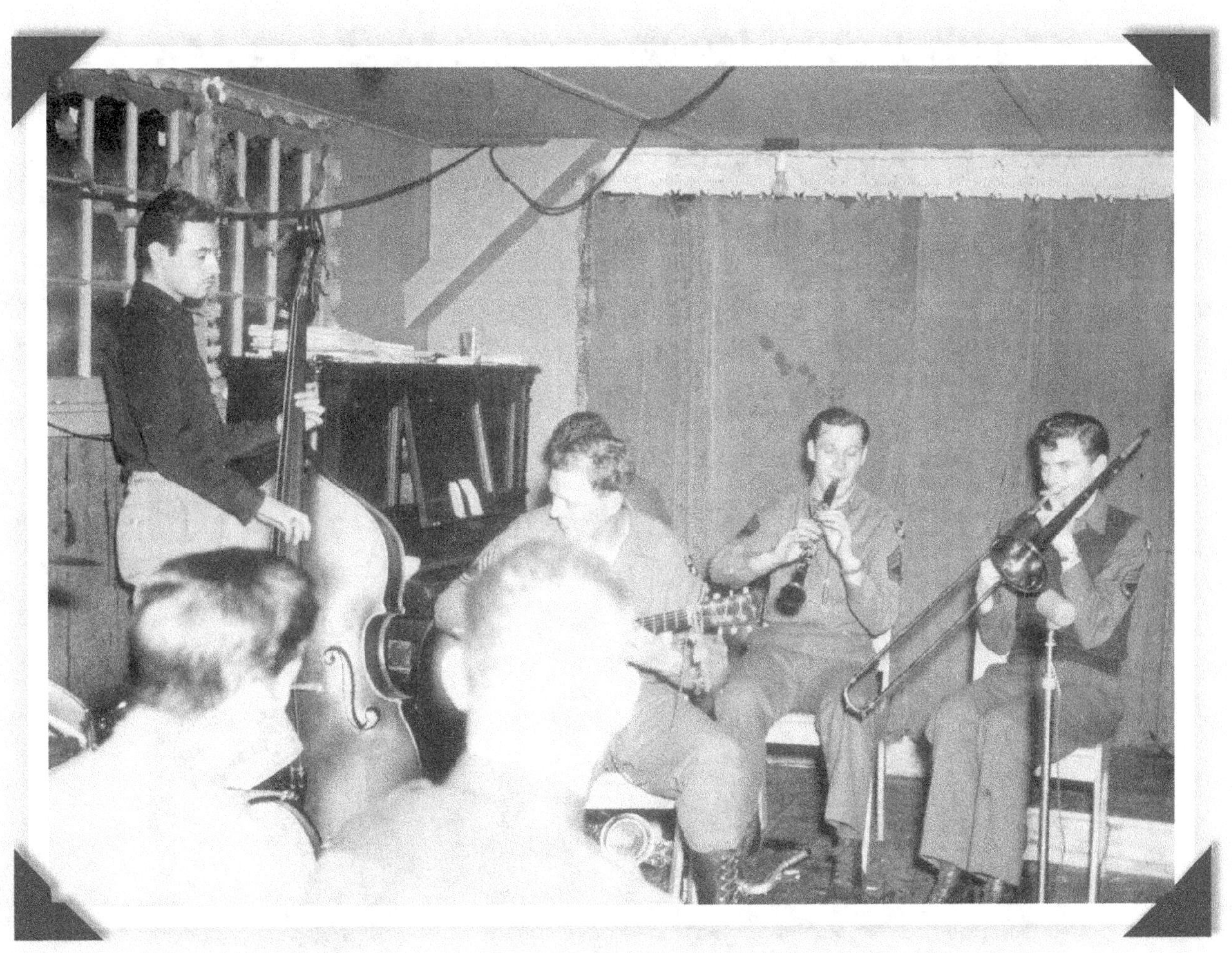

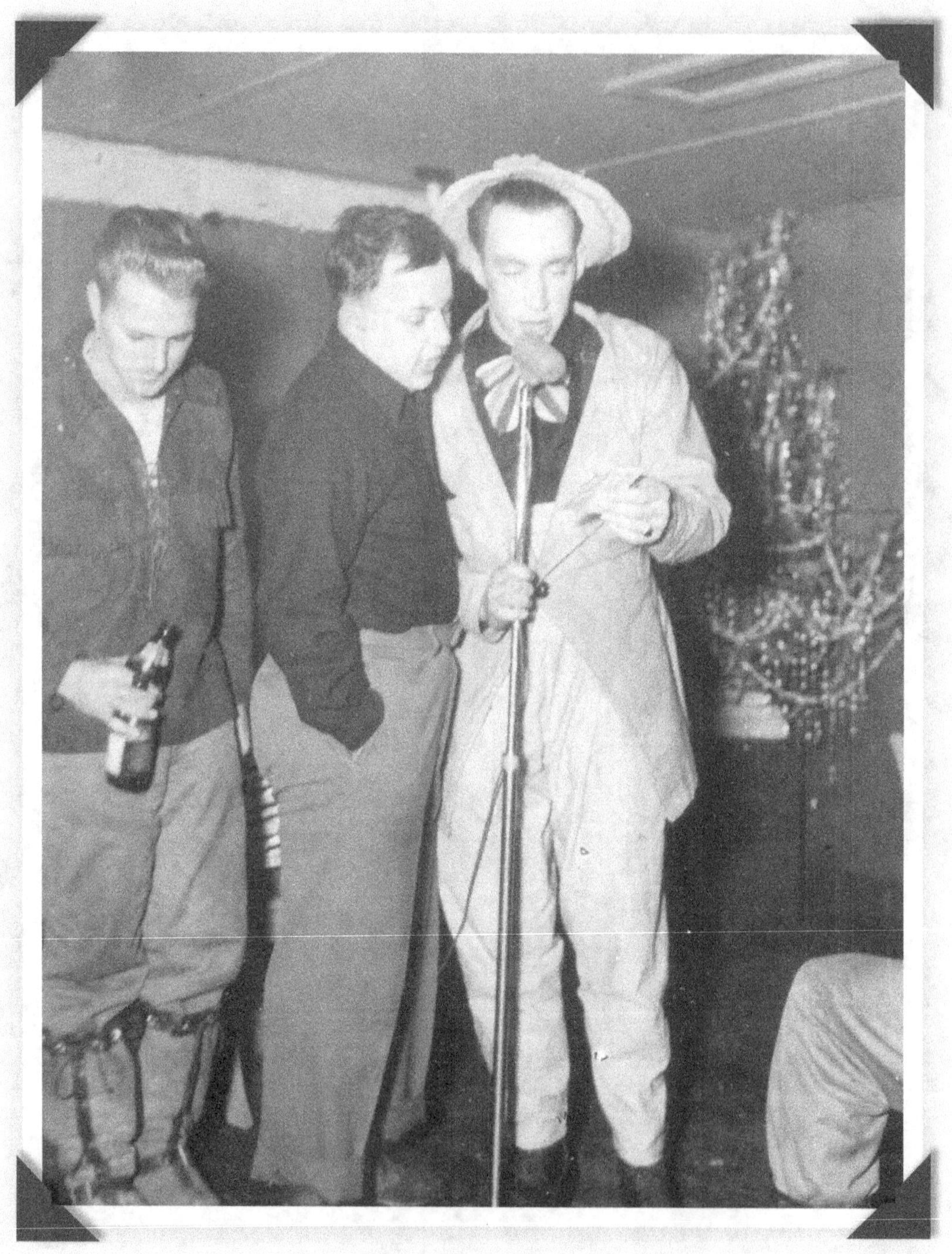

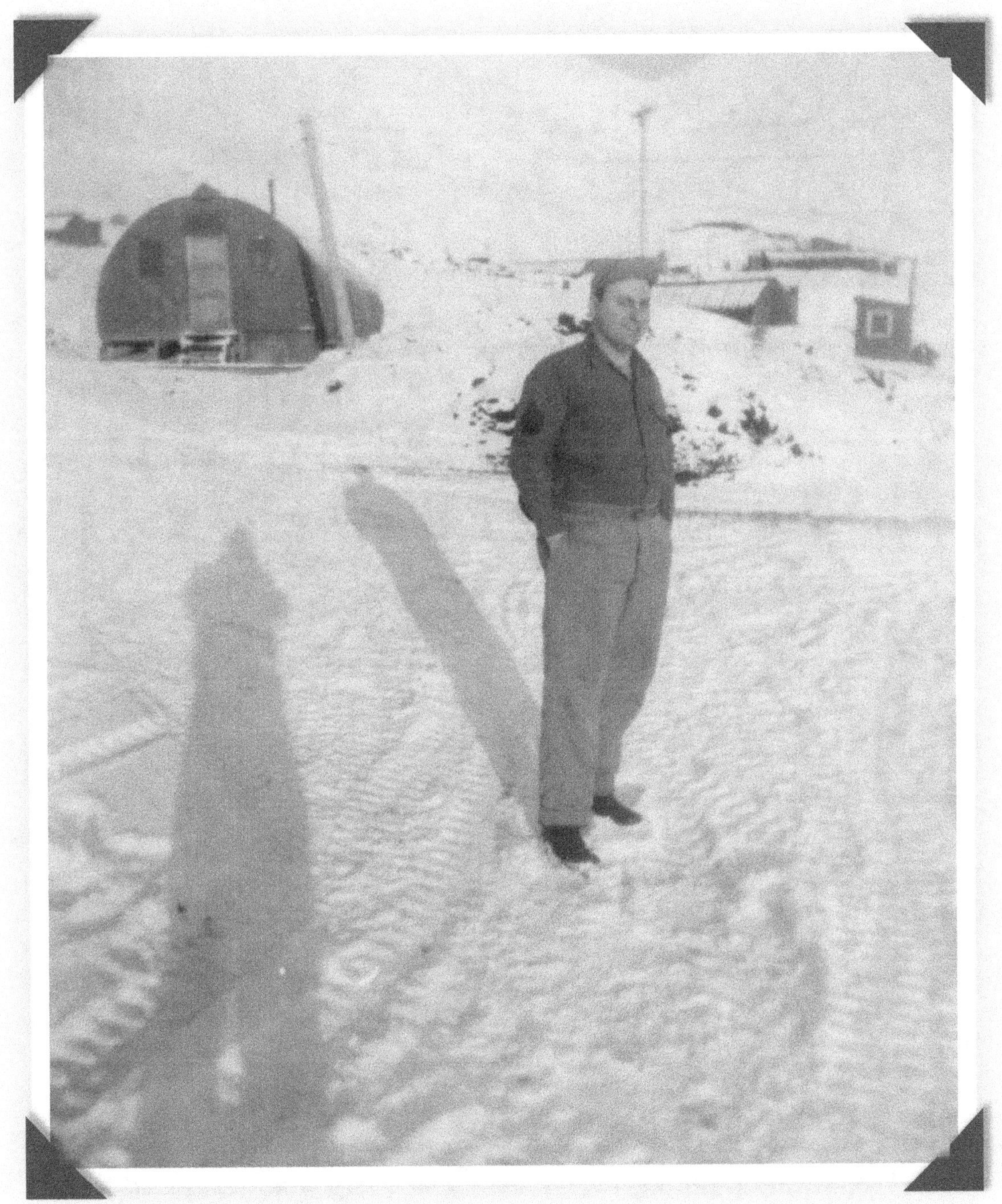

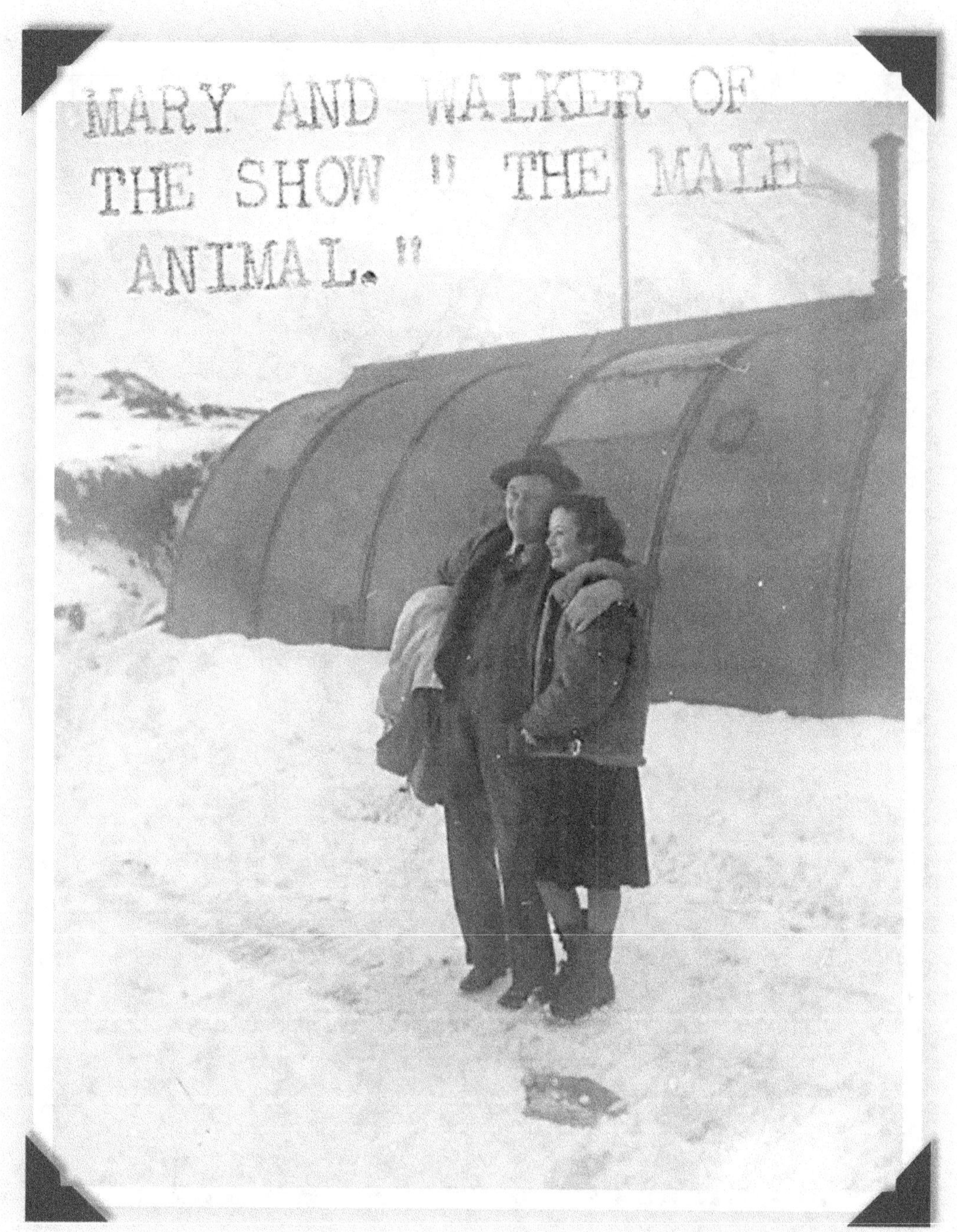

MARY AND WALKER OF
THE SHOW " THE MALE
ANIMAL."

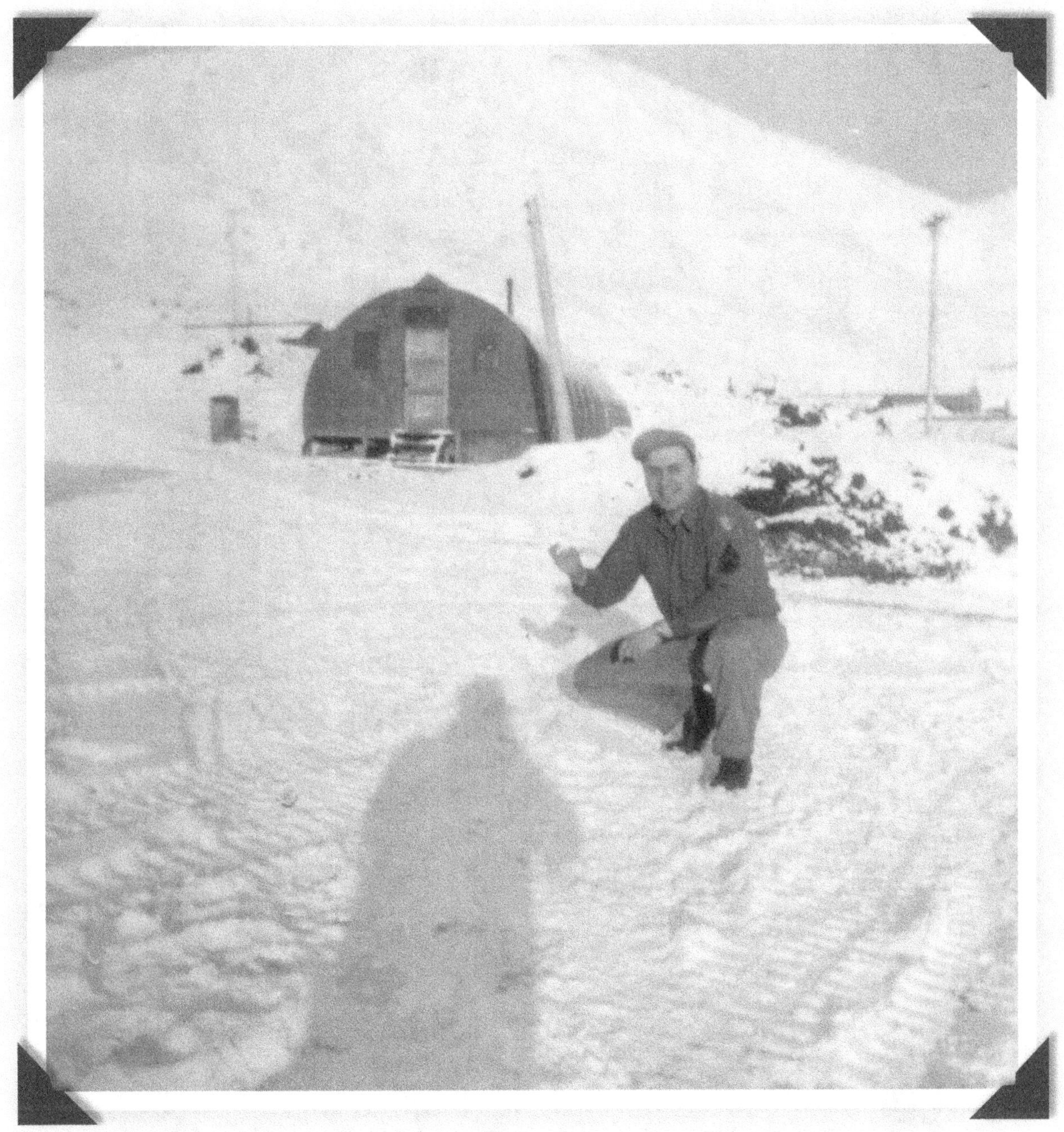

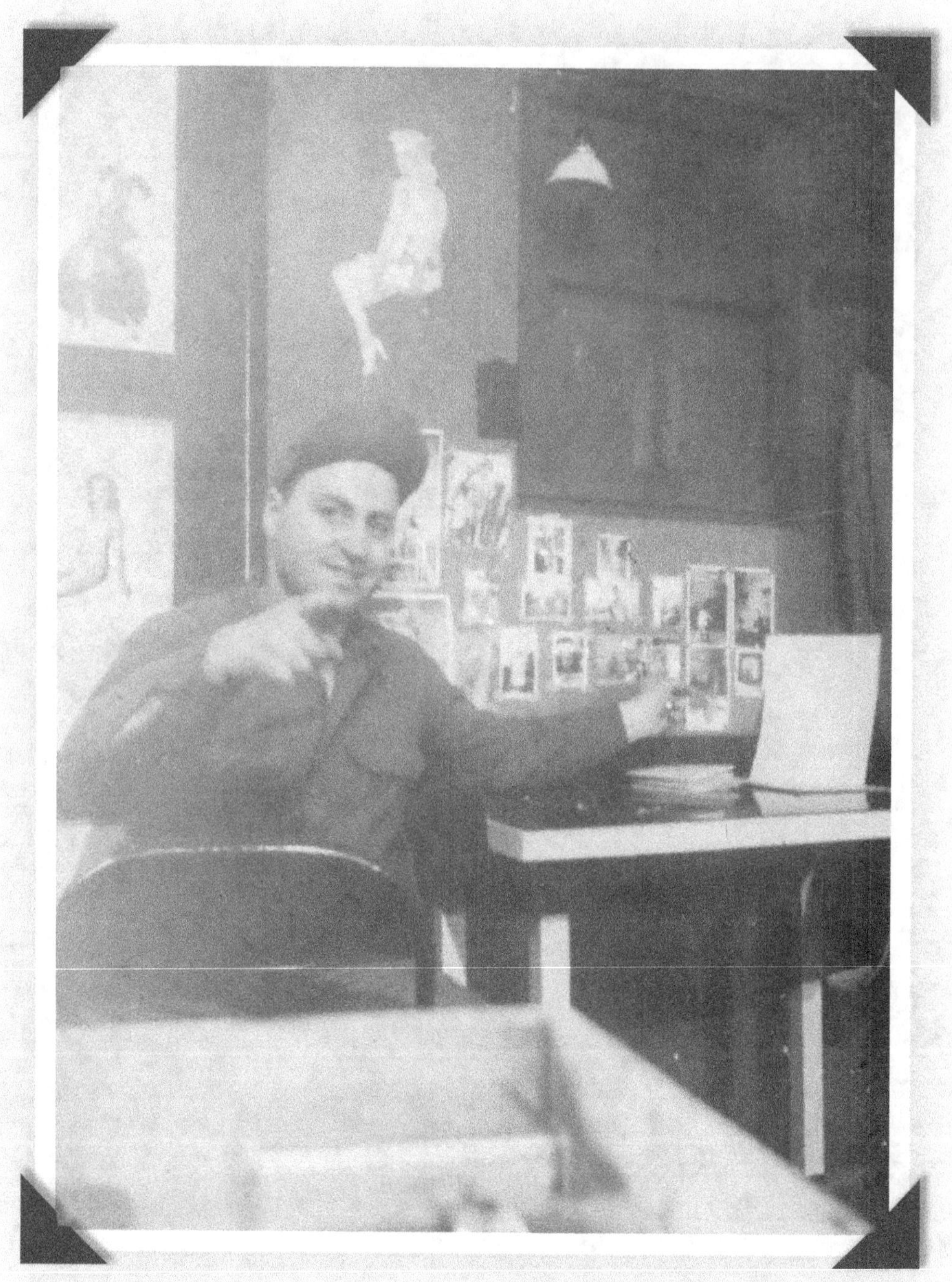

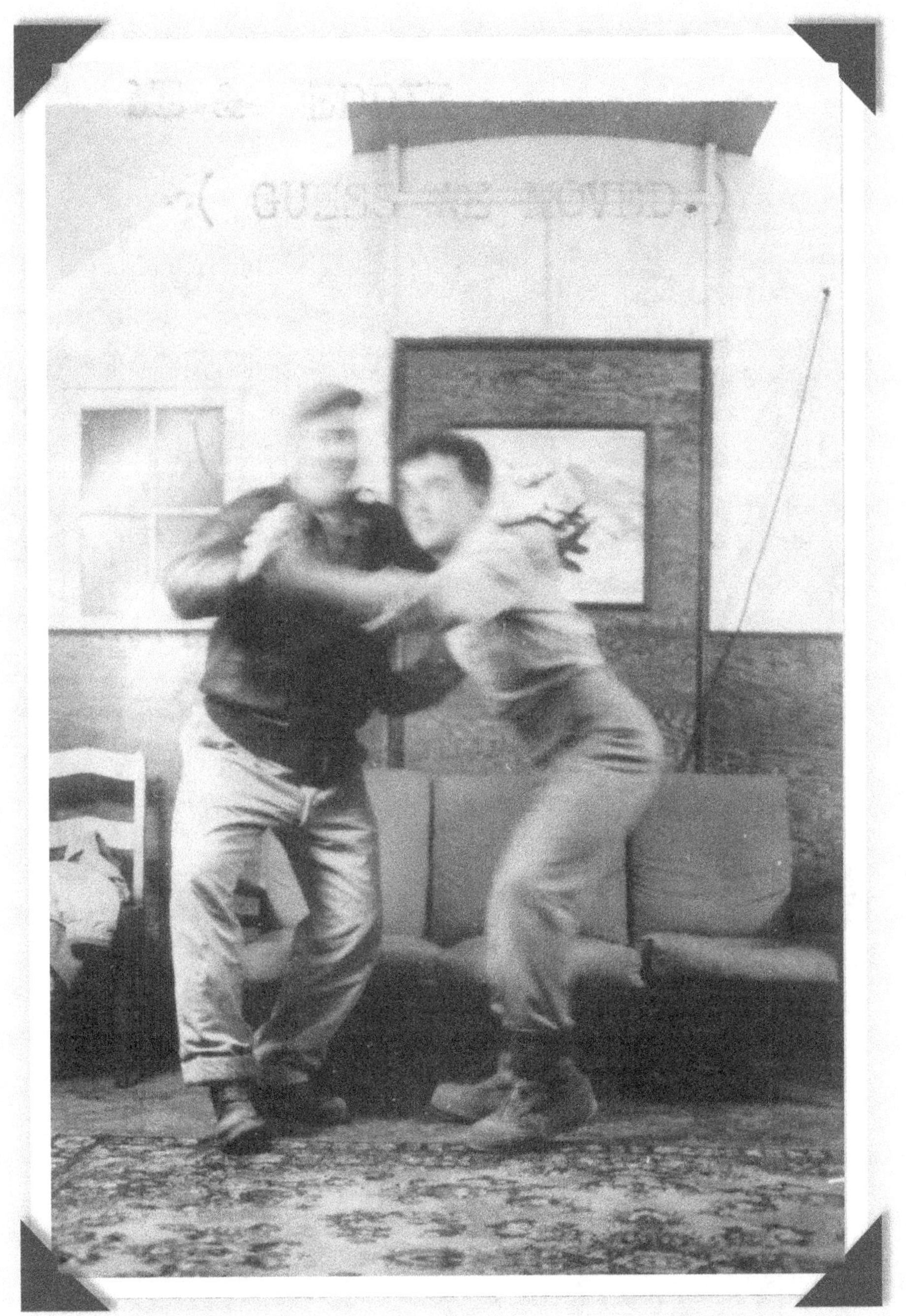

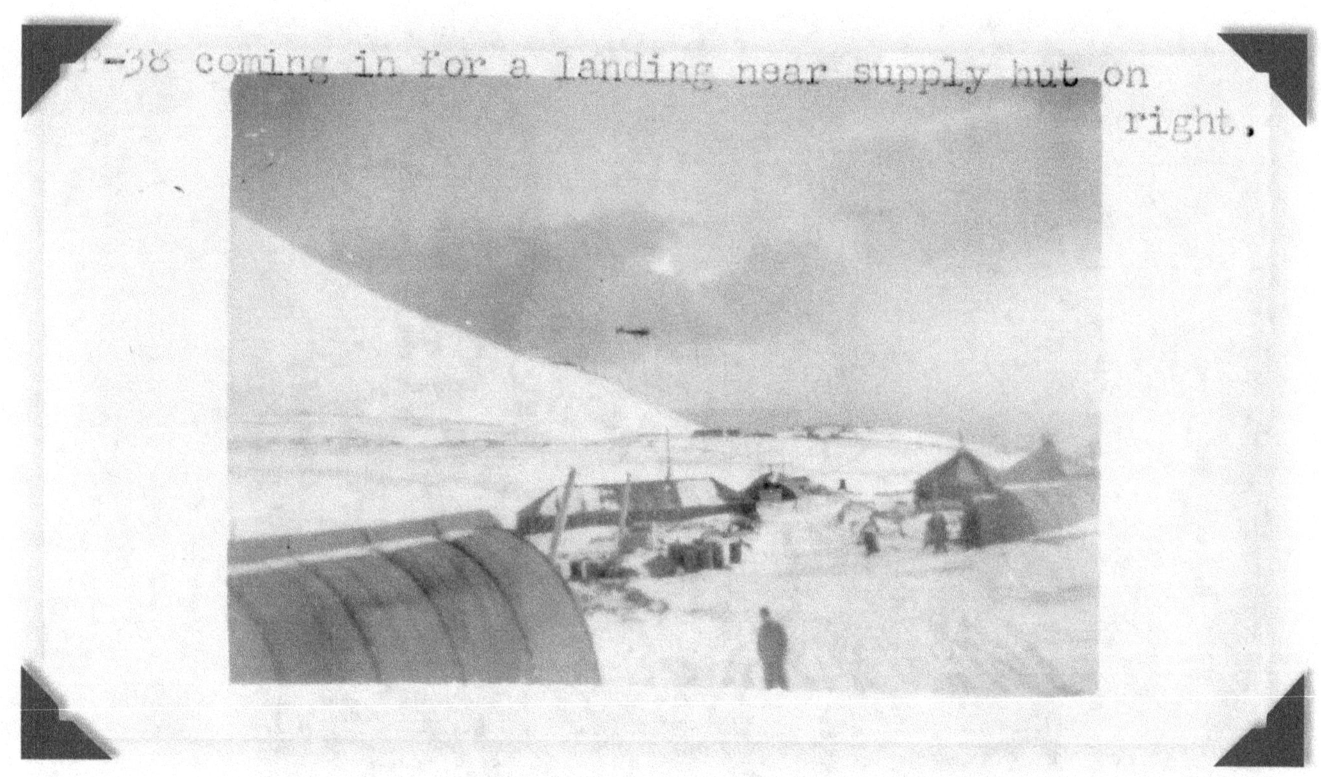
-38 coming in for a landing near supply hut on
right.

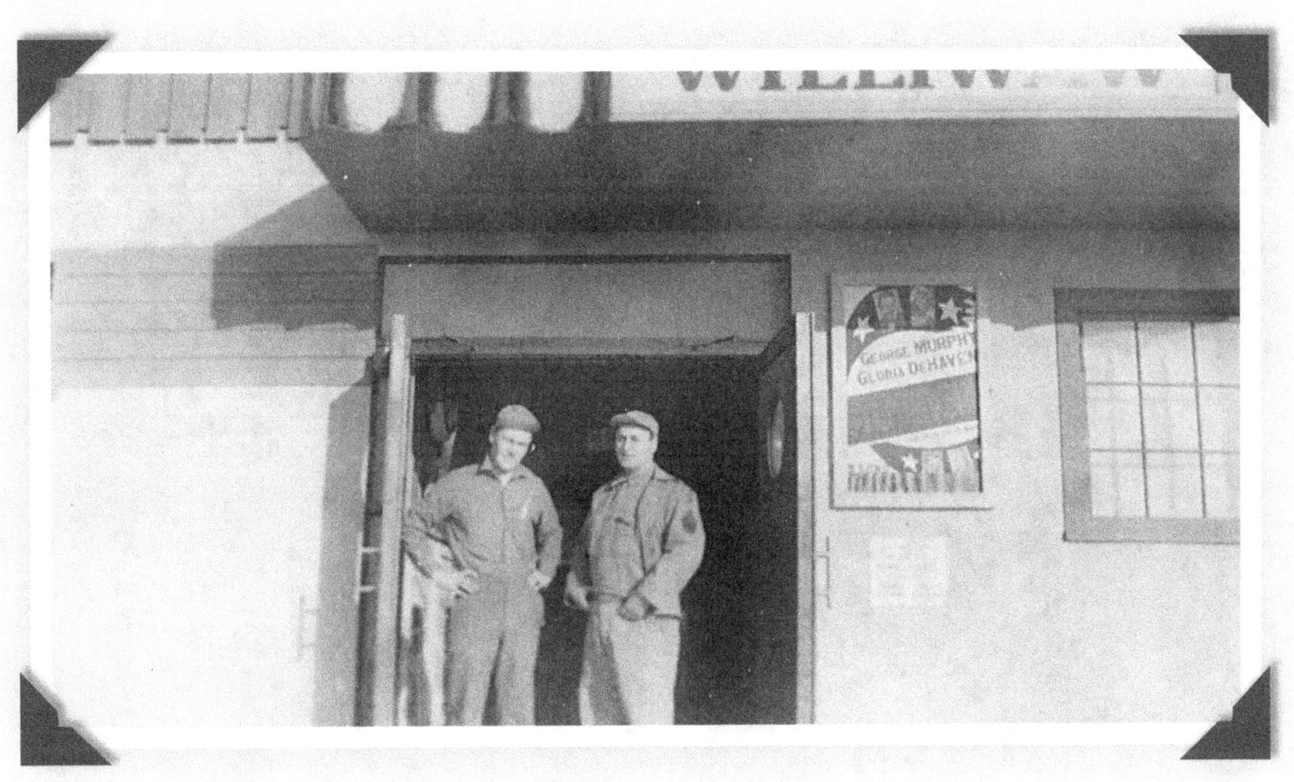

GEORGE MURPHY
GLORIA DeHAVEN

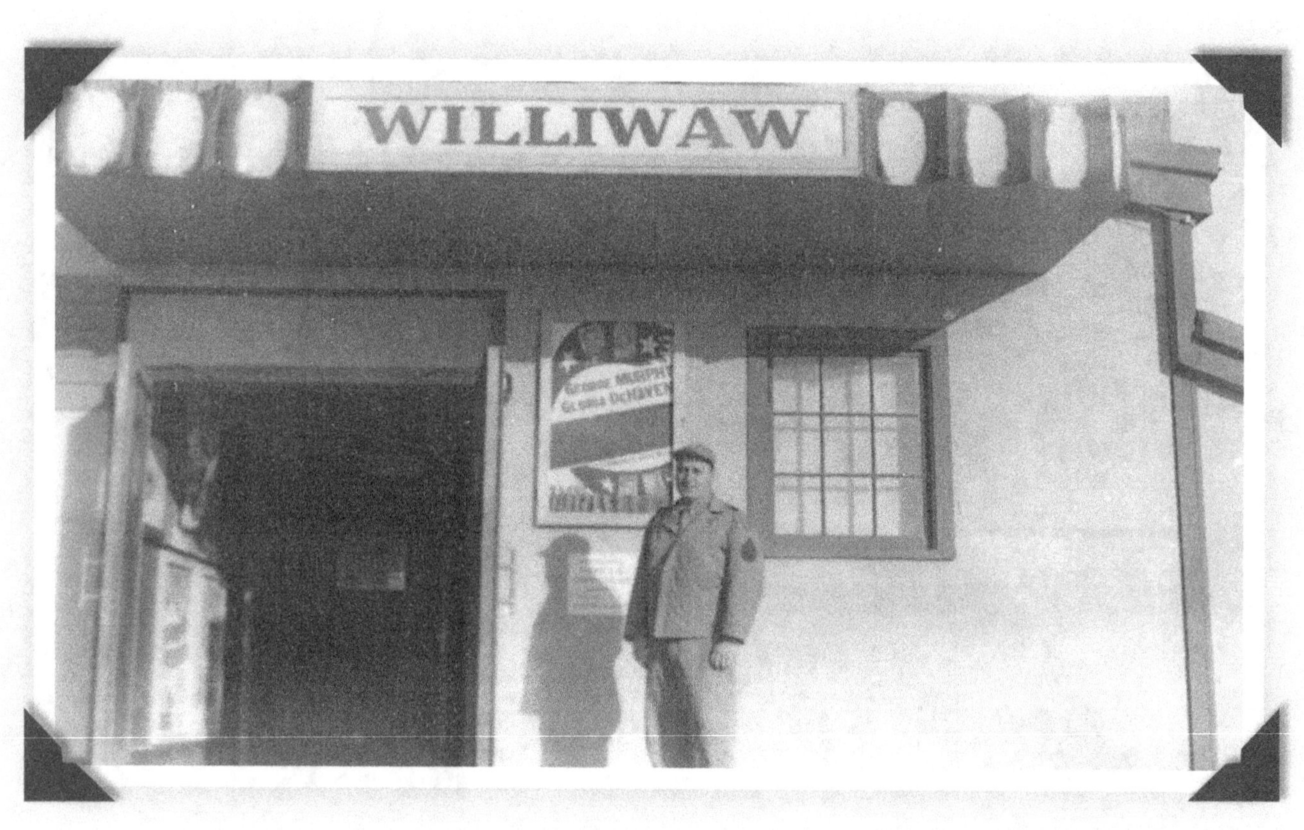

WILLIWAW
GEORGE MURPHY
GLORIA DeHAVEN

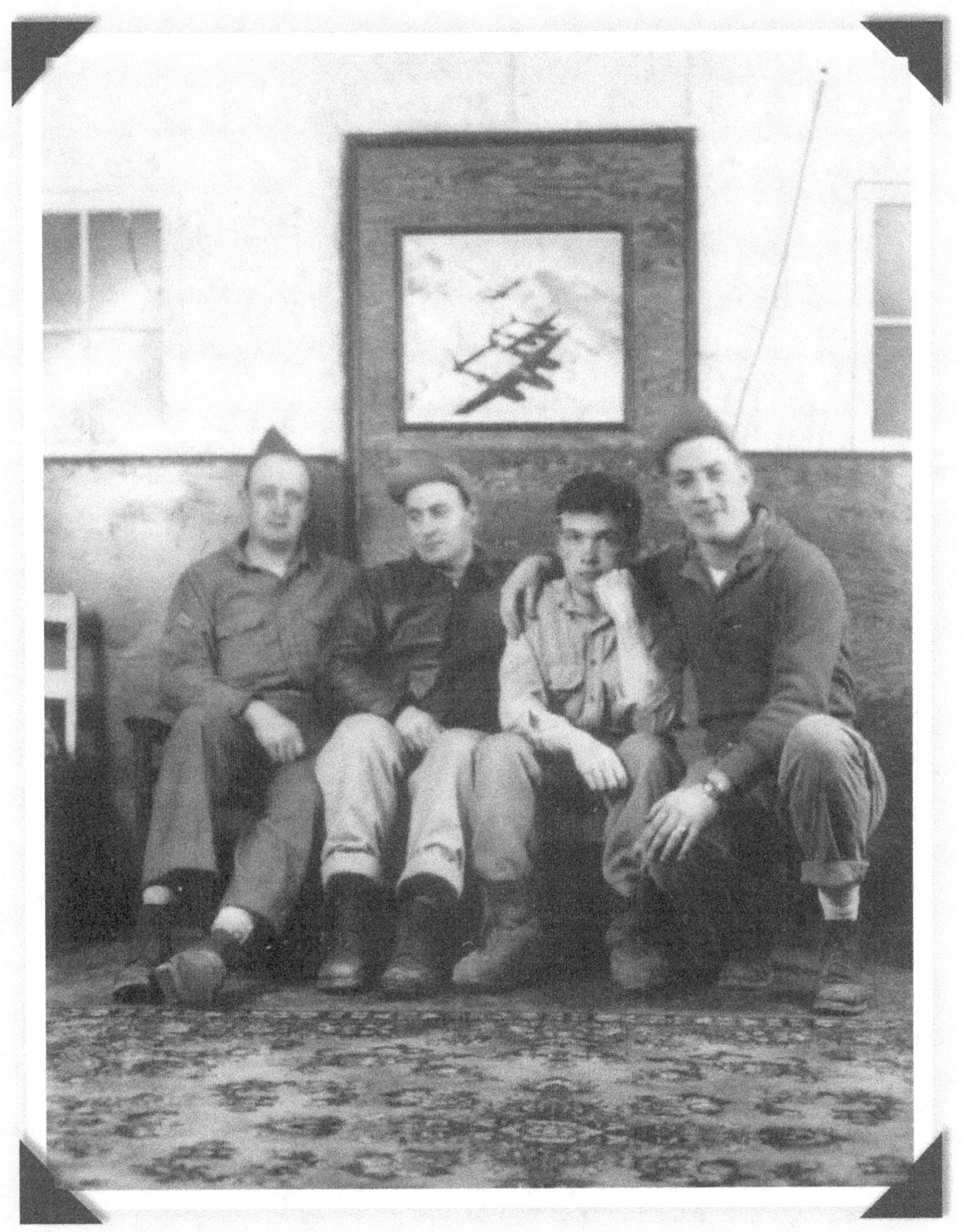

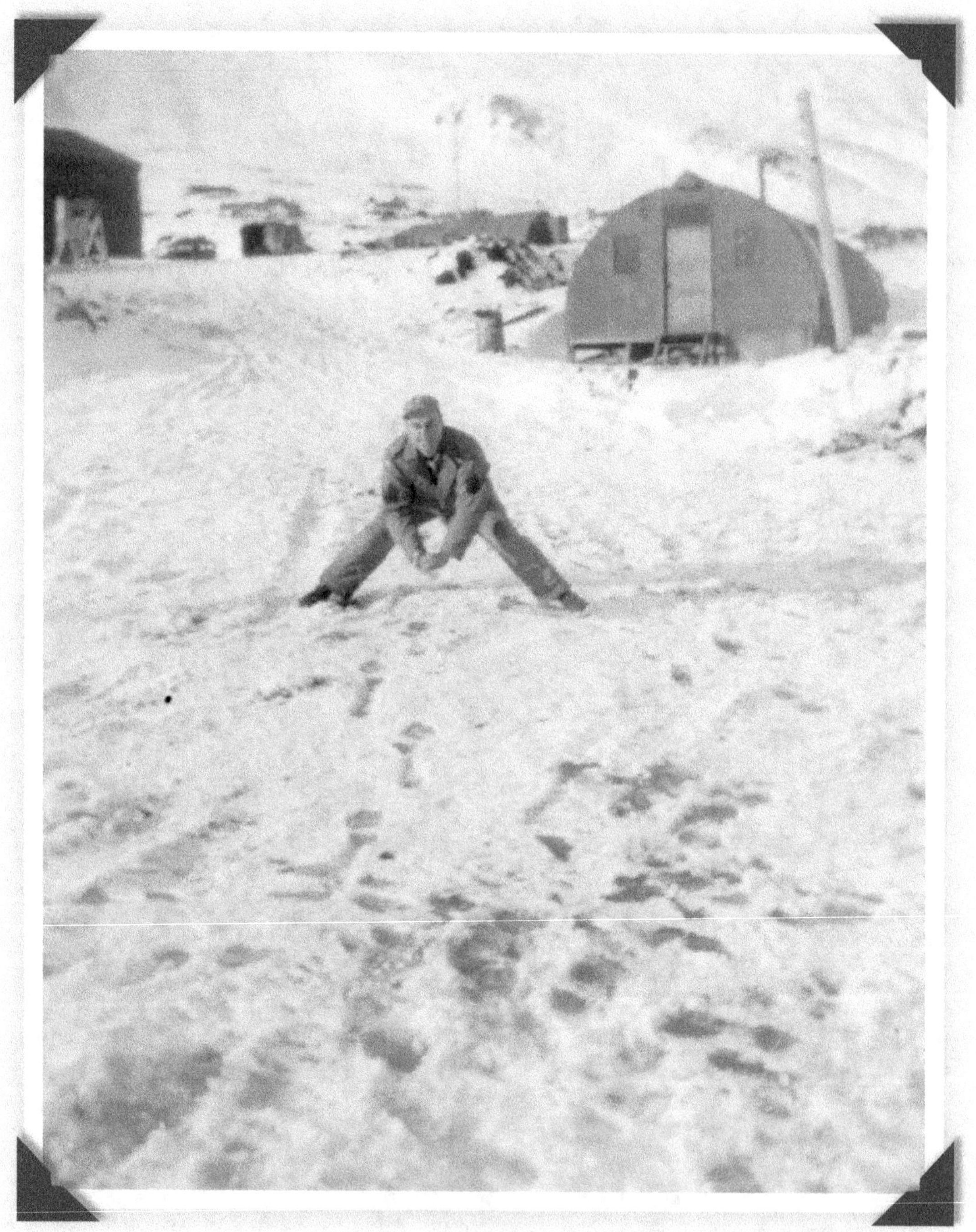

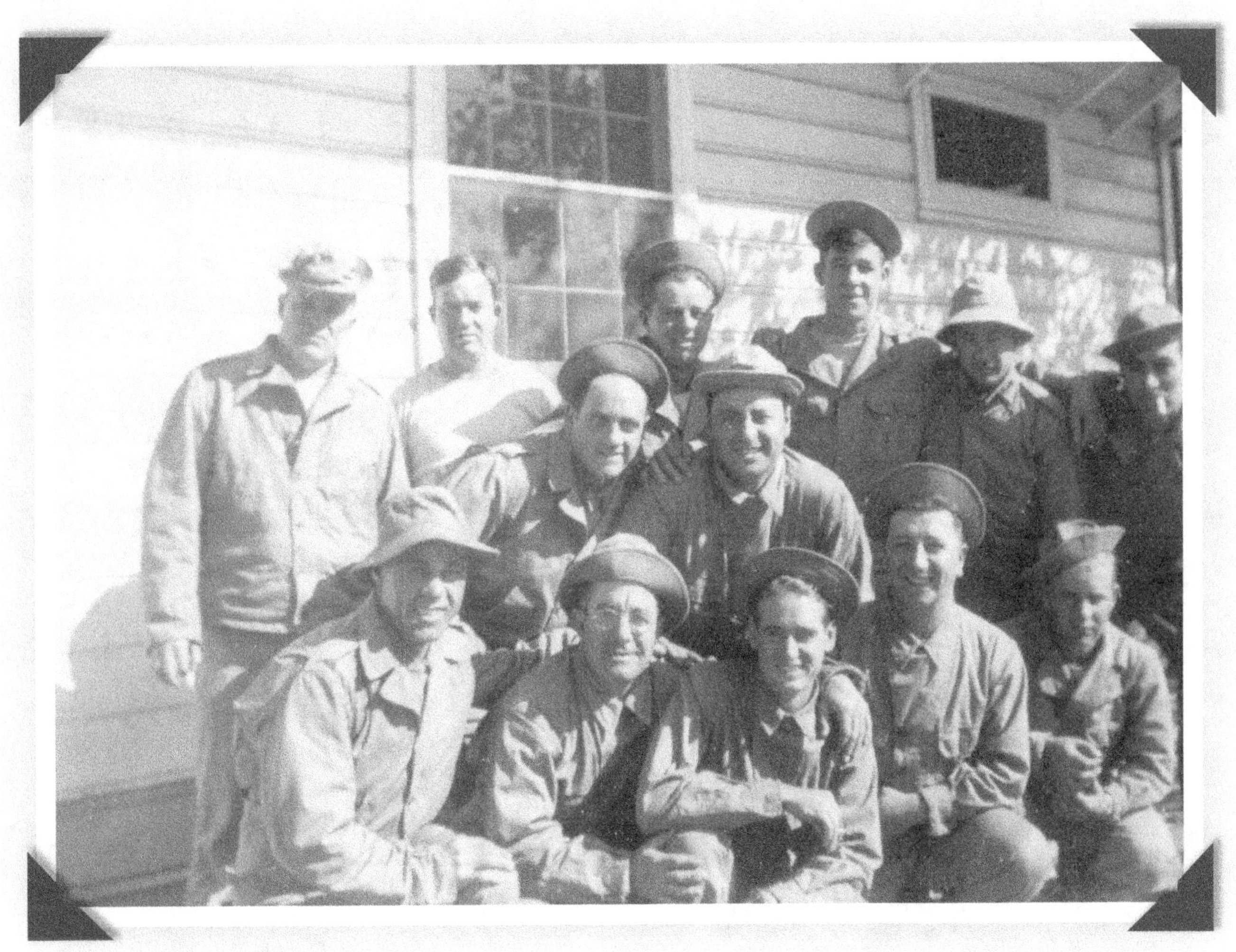

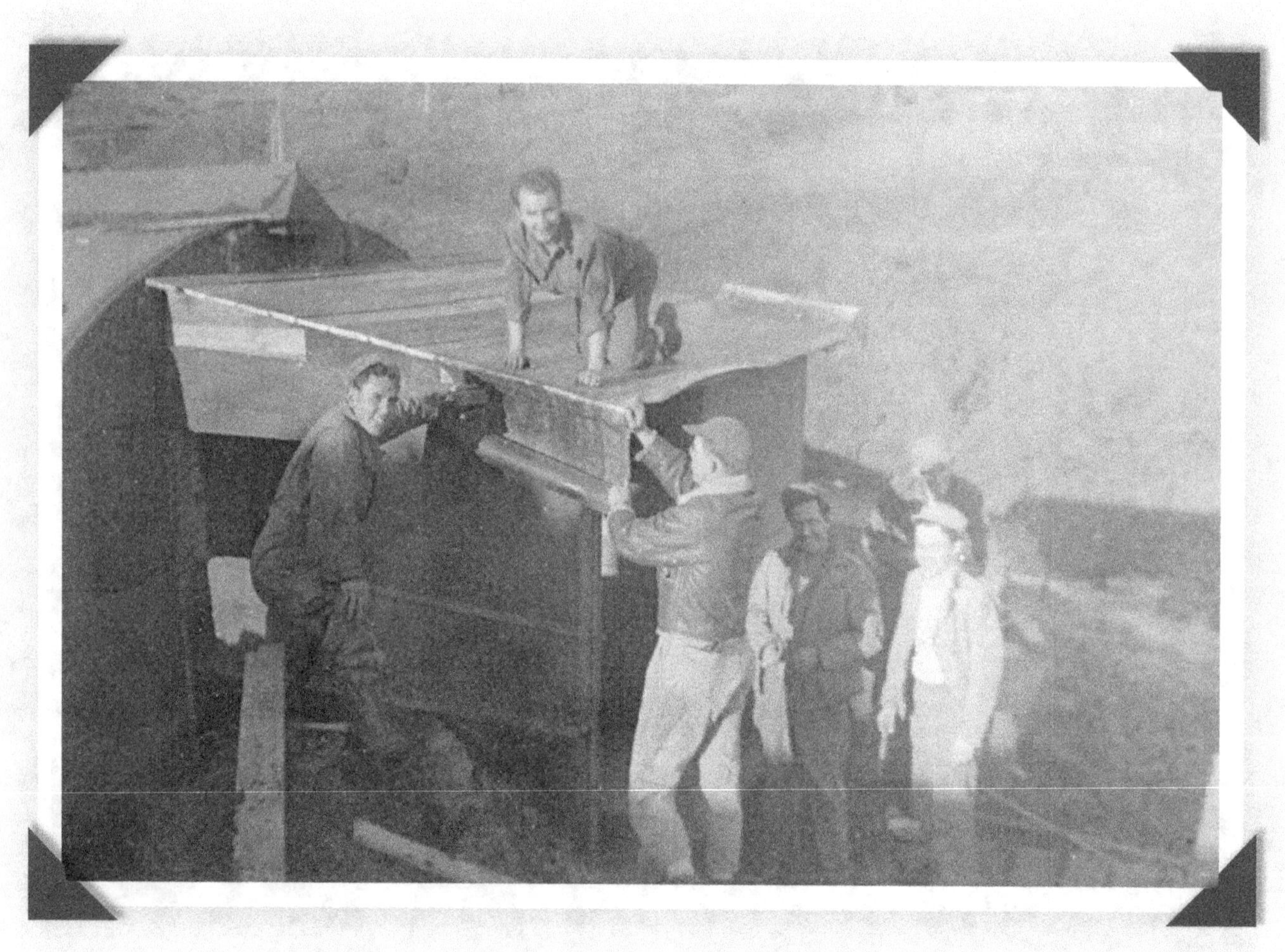

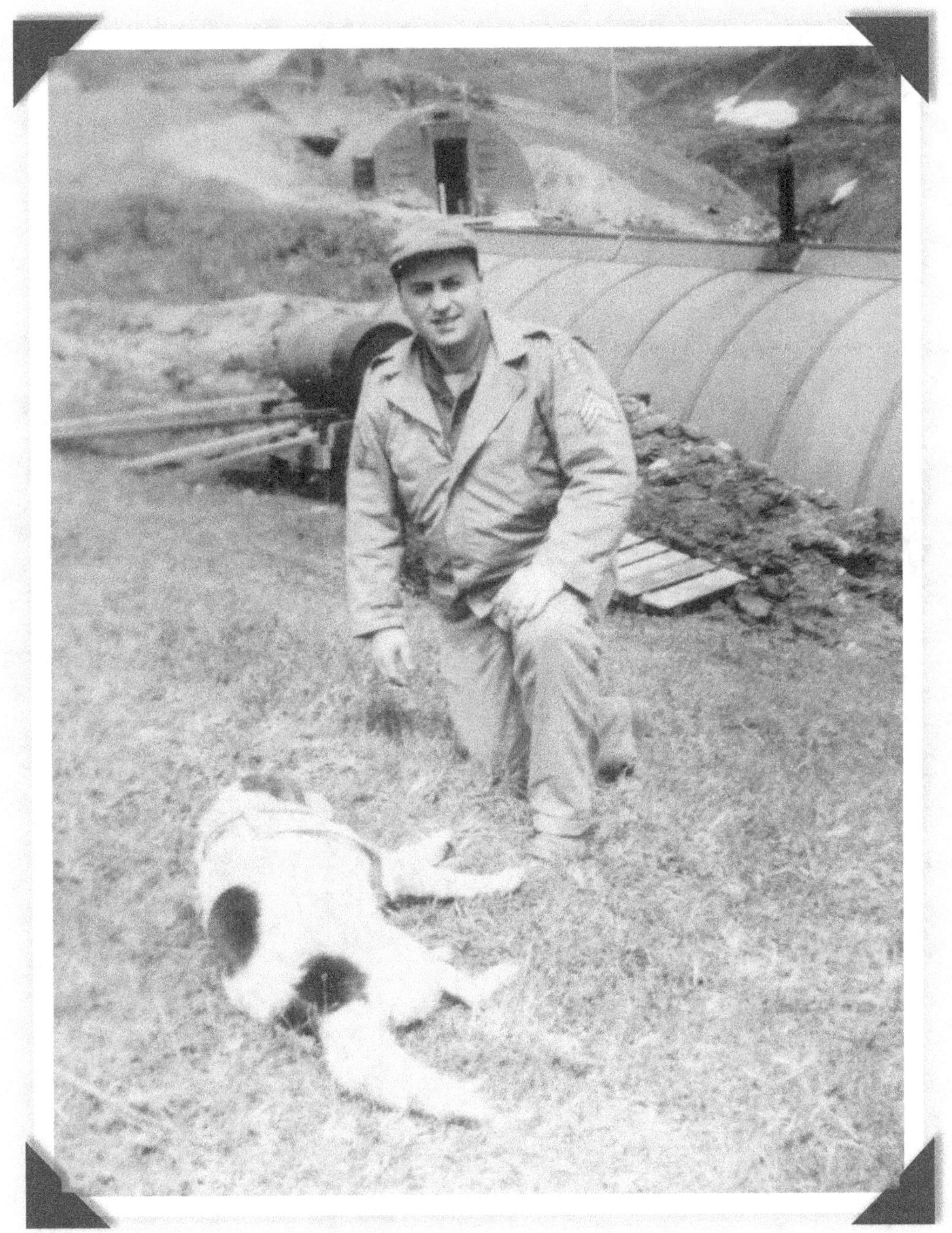

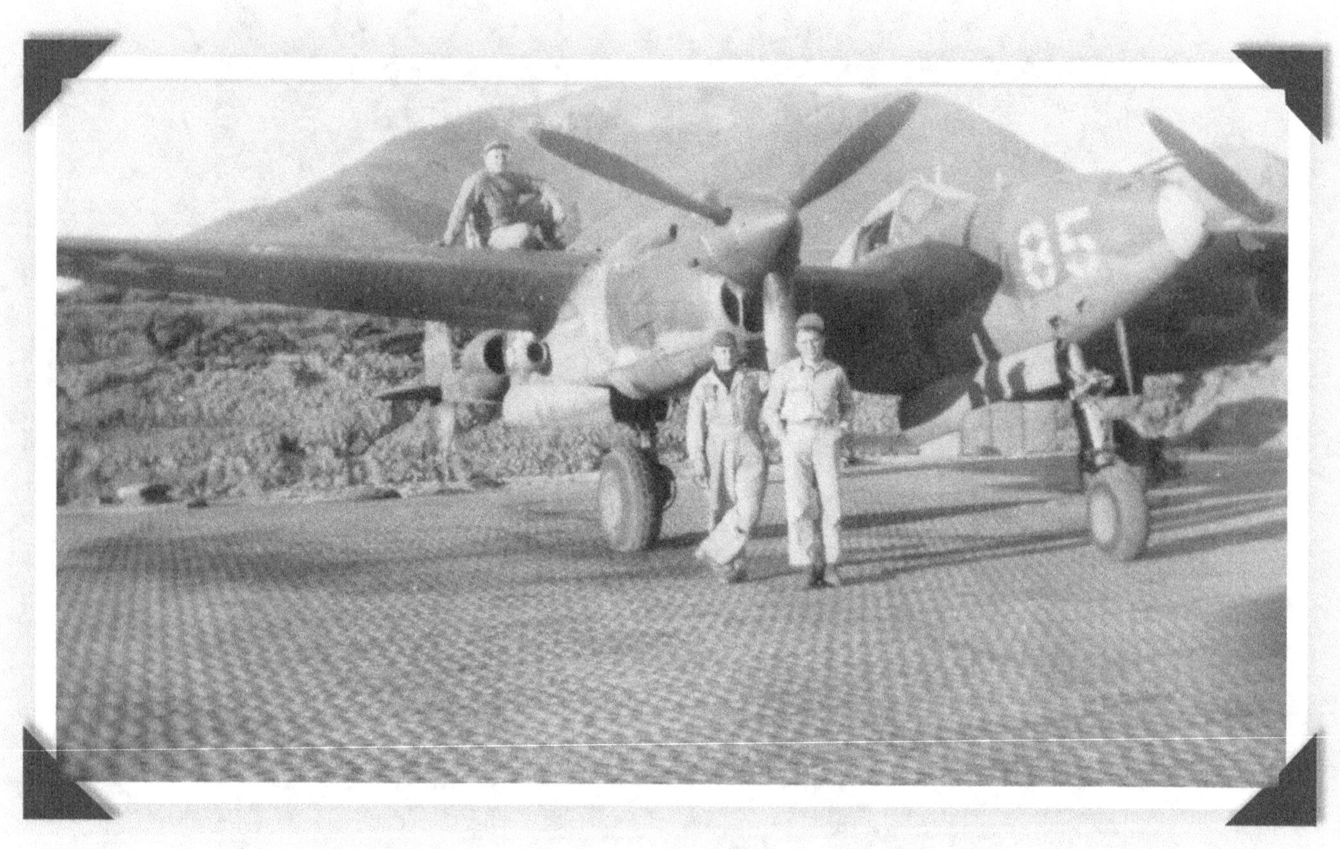

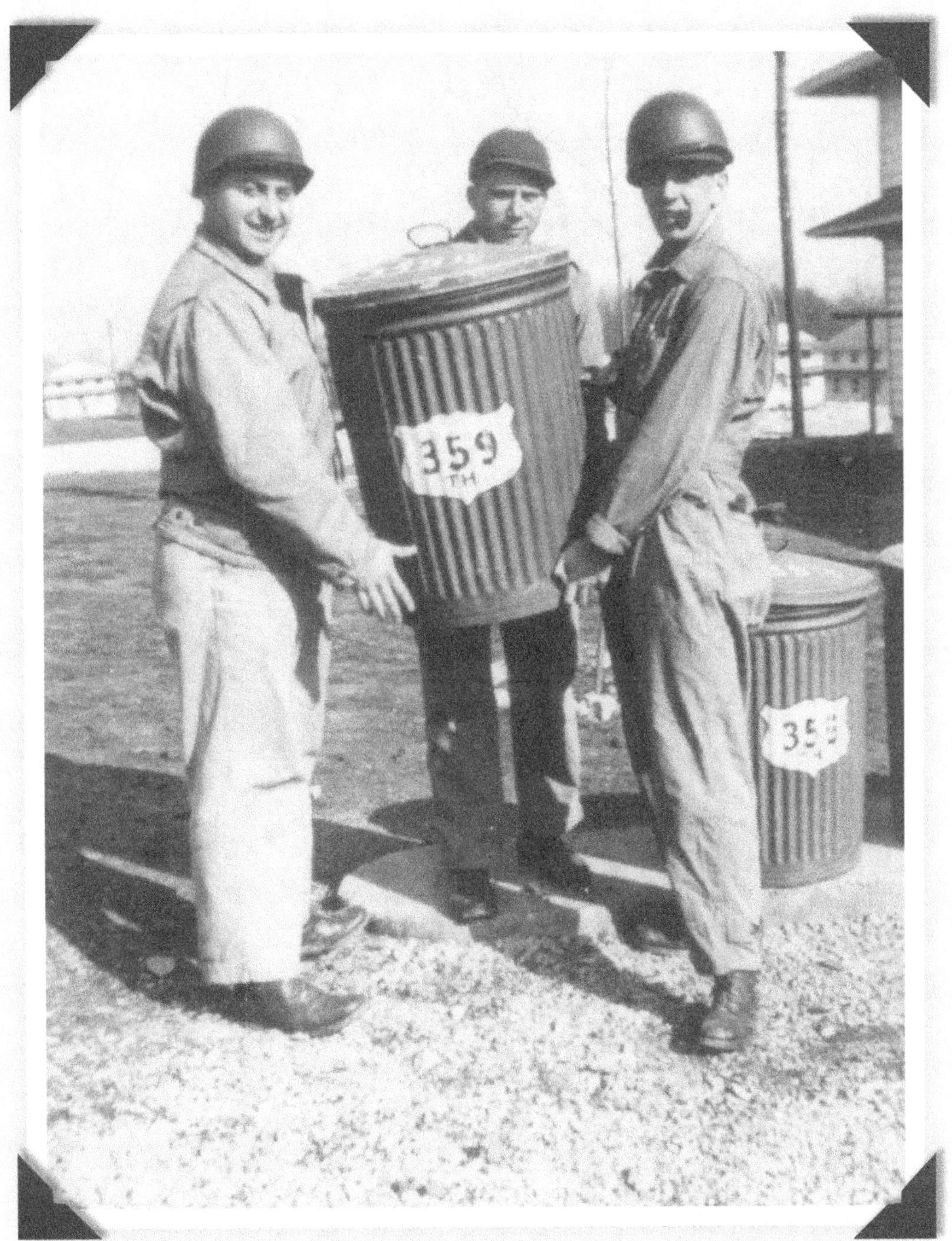
359
TH
359
359

CODA

The years passed quickly.
I live now live in a particular present as a septuagenarian.
Life is good and I am excited to continue the graphic journey.

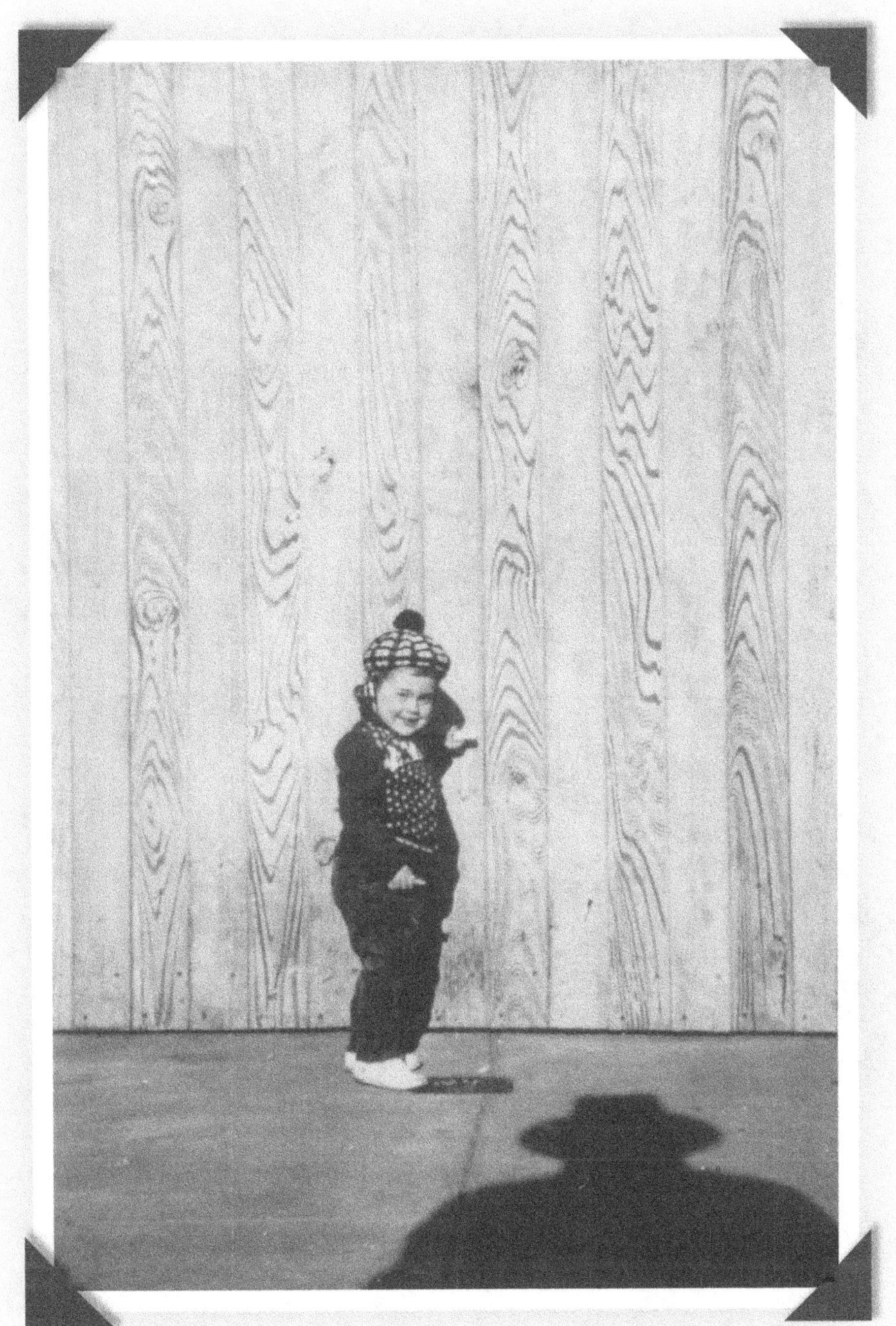

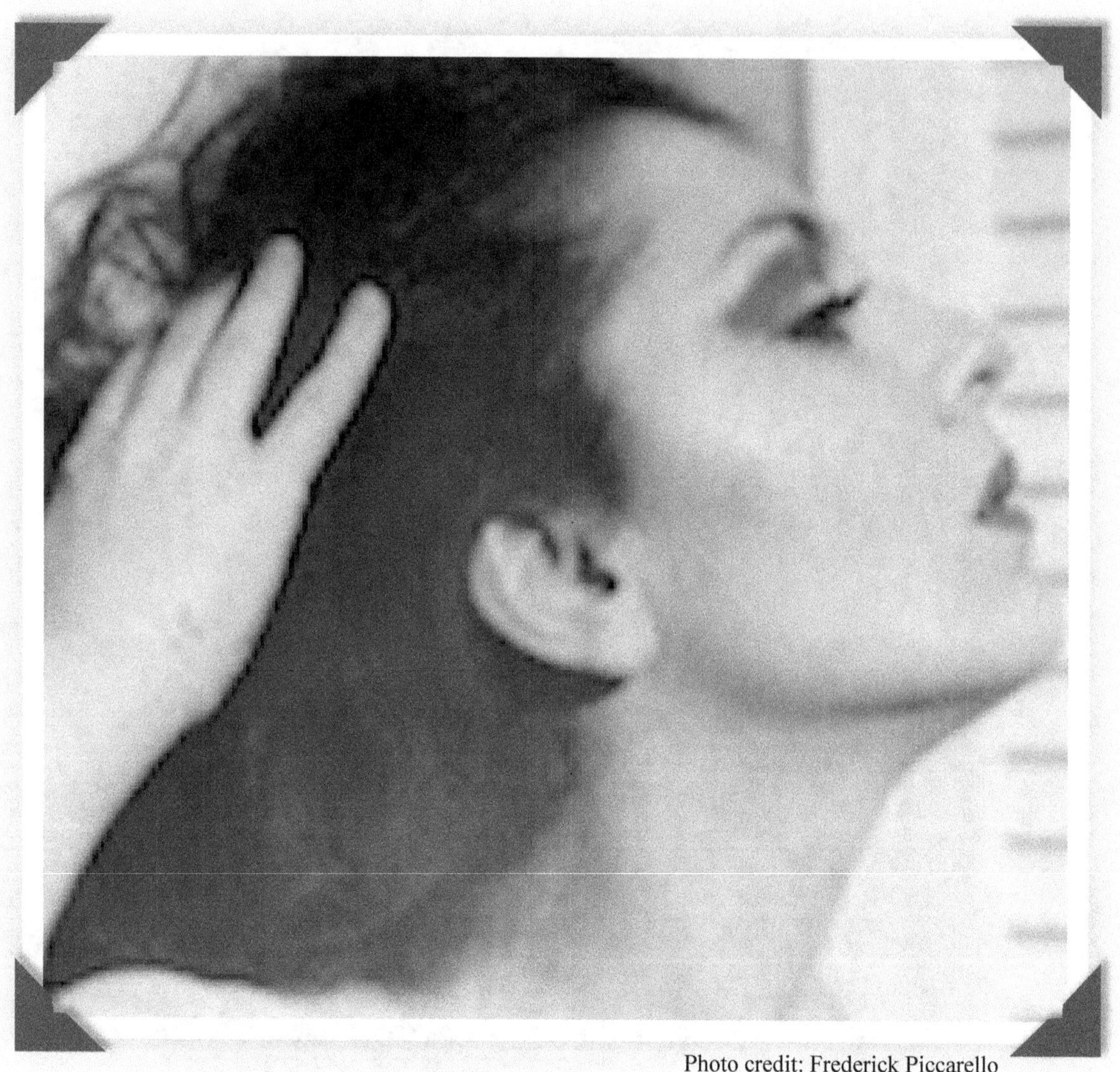

Photo credit: Frederick Piccarello

ABOUT MARJORIE

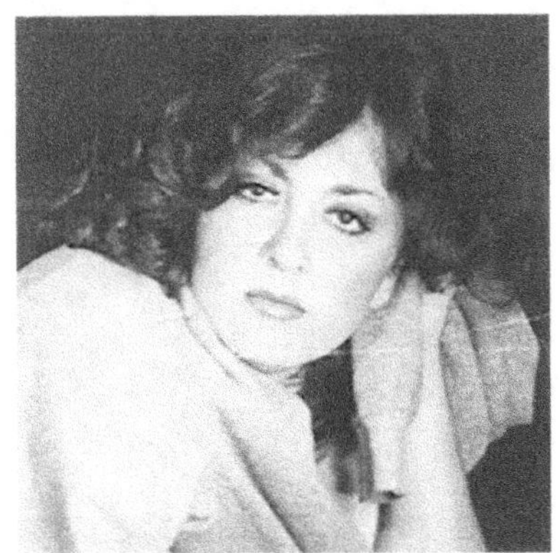

Marjorie J. Levine is a standup comic, an actor, a blogger, an internet broadcaster, and poet. For thirty-five years, she was an elementary school teacher. Her first book of poetry, *ROAD TRIPS*, received rave reviews. That was followed by *the marjorie cartoons*, a quirky compendium of caricatures and witticisms. She lives alone in New York City.